The world's climate has become unstable from global warming. Even though global overheating did not take any leaps, there have been six abrupt shifts since 1976 in other aspects of climate, global in extent. For example, global drought acreage suddenly doubled in 1982 and stayed there. And there have been at least six near-misses. That 12-years-in-36 track record, not computer forecasts, is why we now need a CO_2 cleanup that is big and quick.

Climate surprises are like heart attacks. They occur with little warning. In severity, they range unpredictably from minor to catastrophic—say, failing ecosystems and a human population crash from war, famine, pestilence, and genocide.

Compared to the climate creep from global warming, climate leaps are both sudden and sooner. So our primary concern is no longer about our grandchildren's world, or even our children's. It's about our future—including that of today's seniors.

Books by WILLIAM H. CALVIN

The Great CO2 Cleanup
The Great Climate Leap
Global Fever
Almost Us
A Brief History of the Mind
A Brain for All Seasons
Lingua ex Machina*
The Cerebral Code
How Brains Think
Conversations with Neil's Brain**
How the Shaman Stole the Moon
The Ascent of Mind
The Cerebral Symphony
The River that Flows Uphill
The Throwing Madonna
Inside the Brain**

*with Derek Bickerton
**with George A. Ojemann

THE GREAT CLIMATE LEAP

A Climate Surprise is Like a Heart Attack

WILLIAM H. CALVIN

University of Washington

ClimateBooks

@WilliamCalvin.org

William H. Calvin, Ph.D., is a professor at the University of Washington in Seattle and the author of *Global Fever: How to Treat Climate Change* (University of Chicago Press, 2008) and the award-winning *A Brain for All Seasons: Human Evolution and Abrupt Climate Change* (University of Chicago Press, 2002). Website: WilliamCalvin.org.

Chapters

In memory of climate scientist
STEPHEN H. SCHNEIDER
(1945-2010)

Everyone does something about the weather
but no one talks about it.

— Stephen H. Schneider

A Definition:

Climate is just the long-term view of weather. It's the annual average of temperature and precipitation and winds—as well as their annual highs and lows. When temperature sets a new record high, that's "just weather" the first time it happens— maybe a once-in-500-years event. But when it repeats only a few years later, you start suspecting climate *change*.

The sudden 1982 doubling of the global drought acreage could have been mere weather—except it stayed up near double, never returning to the old 1950-1981 baseline. That's a climate leap on a global scale.

Climate can also creep (what all the talk is about), but it's those climate leaps that tell you something big is happening. And they can cause major damage long before creep gets around to it.

Preface

We are facing a climate catastrophe, one that threatens a human population crash. We must head it off. Here I attempt to define the ballpark in which we are forced to play by the constraints from physics and biology.

Innovation often begins by reframing a problem for which the solution is elusive. That's what I attempt for our climate problem in this short book.

A solution to this reframed problem may come next via recombining old ideas—that's my topic in the second book of the pair, *The Great CO2 Cleanup*.

I'm trying to do a major reframing of how we view the climate threats. That leads to a major reframing of what we should be doing about them—and the relevant time frame for taking effective action. Given the reframing, this short book is a departure from the usual climate books (including my last book, *Global Fever*).

The biggest danger is from sudden climate leaps, not the gradual transitions; it's the difference between hitting a brick wall and gradually slowing to a stop. Given six sudden shifts since

1976, global in scale, the playing field's boundaries are seen to be measured in decades, not centuries.

Thus I focus on

- climate instabilities such as the sudden doubling of the worldwide drought acreage in 1982, not on gradual overheating per se;

- on catastrophic endpoints such as a human population crash, not on the spiraling cost of summer air-conditioning; and

- on the need for a short-term massive cleanup of CO_2, not on the emission reductions needed for the long term.

1
An Inventory of Trouble

You may congratulate yourself if you already know that we are in the midst of a climate crisis that began with pickaxe-level technologies for burning fossil fuels *and* clearing forests (take 5 points for each). Both increase the **carbon dioxide (CO2 hereafter)** in the air, trapping more of the sun's heat and thereby overheating the Earth.

Knew that? Take another 5, and 5 for each of the following aspects of *climate creep.*

- Did you know that global overheating causes the excess of high winds, deluge, drought, and forest fires—not just heat waves?

- Subtract 5 points if you thought that heavier snowstorms meant that global warming wasn't happening. Deluge includes heavier snowstorms because there is more moisture in the air to turn into snow, thanks to more evaporation from warmer tropical oceans.

- And know that global warming is not uniform? That since 1977, the land has warmed twice as fast[1] as the oceans? And that the enhanced temperature contrast over coastlines rearranges circulation paths as the stronger on-shore winds punch through old barriers?

- Did you already know that, as the highly-reflective sea ice disappears, to be replaced by dark sea surface, the Arctic Ocean will absorb much more heat each year?

- That this regional warming in the Arctic will release CO_2 and methane (the principal ingredient of natural gas, many times more potent as a greenhouse gas than CO_2) as the tundra thaws, thereby amplifying the anthropogenic warming?

- Did you already know that fossil fuel CO_2 emissions rose 3 percent annually since 2003—in spite of international efforts such as the Kyoto Protocol? That, if continued until 2023, our annual emissions will be double those of 2000?

- Did you understand that "stabilizing" emissions merely stops the 3% annual *growth* in emissions, much as limiting the annual number of trucks allowed into a garbage dump still allows the pile to grow? That even zero emissions (closing the CO_2 dump) will still leave us with the accumulated excess CO_2 and its climate impacts for many centuries?

- Subtract 5 points if you thought that reducing CO_2 emissions (a rate of addition) would soon reduce atmospheric CO_2 (the accumulated quantity) and climate problems. (It's like confusing miles per hour with the miles yet to travel.)

If your score is up to 45 by now, you are well-informed about climate *creep*.

There are also *climate leaps*—abrupt climate shifts. Abruptness often does far more damage than a slow creep to the same endpoint would have done.

Climate surprises are like heart attacks. They occur with little warning. They range unpredictably from minor to catastrophic. Compared to the climate creep from global warming, climate surprises are both sudden and sooner.

Five points each if, in addition to the usual prehistoric examples from ice cores[2], you've heard of these recent examples of climate leap:

- The global acreage in extreme drought doubled in just a year's time with the big 1982 El Niño—and stayed latched up near double for the next fifteen years, even during three La Niñas[3].

- Global drought then leaped to nearly triple the 1950-1982 baseline with the even bigger 1997 El Niño, suddenly dropping back to double[4] in 2005.

- That even rain forests burned extensively in 1997-1998? Had that oversized El Niño lasted a second year, the excess CO_2 in the air could have jumped 50 percent via the burning and rotting of the huge rainforest biomass in Amazonia and Southeast Asia[5].

- By the end of the merely-medium-sized 2002-2005 El Niño, the Amazon rain forests were even more flammable than at the end of the 1997-1998 El Niño, another near miss for "burn locally, crash globally."

Amazonia then set a new record for flammability in 2010[6].

Furthermore, we twice lost an important safety margin. The warm water that splits off from the Gulf Stream loop west of Ireland to become the Norwegian Current serves to heat the frigid Canadian winds before they reach Europe. This tropical water, having lost its heat via evaporation but retained its salt, normally sinks via whirlpools to the bottom of the Greenland Sea north of Iceland, making room for more warm surface water to flow into high northerly latitudes.

- Did you realize that this Greenland Sea flushing[7] failed in 1978, recovering over the following decade?

- Or that the second largest flushing site, in the Labrador Sea[8], failed in 1997? Flushing resumed in the winter of 2007-2008. Were both major sites to fail, there would be a climate leap within several years as sea surface temperature cooled and winds rearranged.

- Subtract 20 points if you thought that the remaining uncertainties in temperature measurement meant that all of the aforementioned climate change isn't a problem. The global mean temperature is mostly an indicator like the stock market indices, not where the action is—say, sudden circulation shifts over continents from the growing temperature *difference* between ocean and land.

The final section concerns what you know about plans to act against climate creep and climate leap.

You may have noticed that most action proposals focus on *mitigation* ("softening the blow" in policyspeak; things such as slowing down emissions growth via shifts to clean energy and electric cars). Our current climate response is mostly a re-emphasis of the old virtues—clean air, clean energy, sustainable agriculture, reforestation, greater efficiency, less waste, longer-term thinking—few of which will help us quickly recover from our current 40 percent excess of CO_2.

While long overdue and still needed for the long run, mere emissions reduction is now analogous to locking the barn door after the horse is gone—not likely to recover the horse, though giving the appearance of taking action.

Besides mitigation, there's *adaptation* (say, living in caves where it is cooler, literally making us troglodytes).

Seldom mentioned, even by climate scientists, is the third obvious action: actually *repairing climate* itself and thereby backing out of the danger zone.

Do you understand (5 points each) these aspects of climate action?

- That serious emissions reduction only delays the 2°C overheating in the US by nine years[9], from 2028 to 2037?

- That even if developed countries stopped emitting CO_2, developing countries would likely burn their own coal and

oil for many decades in order to modernize with
electricity and personal vehicles?

- That even achieving zero emissions globally would still
  result in severe climate problems for centuries, that one-
  fourth of the excess CO_2 will still remain in the air for
  more than a thousand years?

- That the oceans will absorb one-third of the excess
  atmospheric CO_2, thereby causing the acidification of the
  ocean surface? That we'd then have a second crisis
  because of killing off the bottom of the food chain?

- Subtract 5 points if you thought that "stabilizing CO_2" was
  the same thing as fixing an unstable climate.

- That the only intervention likely to back us out of the
  current danger zone for creep, leap, and acidification is to
  remove the excess CO_2 already in the air?

A large climate leap could destroy civilization by triggering a
human population crash via famine, pestilence, war, and
genocide. This could happen long before climate creep by itself
could cause such catastrophes. Another abrupt climate shift could
happen next year, not just in our children's lifetimes, and, like
heart attacks, it might be much larger than previous ones.

Brushing your teeth more regularly is not a fix for a cavity
that has already developed. Our current emissions-reduction
agenda now requires an emergency fix to make the long-term

view relevant again. To speak only of *emissions reduction* is like preaching fire prevention to the four-alarm fire down the block.

Thanks to fifty years of inaction since the first scientific warning to policymakers (aided by the unscrupulous promotion of denial and delay), our biggest problem is no longer future emissions and climate creep. It is the excess CO_2 we already have and the climate leaps that have already begun.

We dare not wait for better understanding before acting. It's clear that the planetary emergency has already arrived—and that only swift action to recapture past emissions can be an effective treatment.

2
Discovering Global Fever

You can't say I wasn't warned. When I was in the sixth grade (that's back in 1950) in Kansas City, we got the *Saturday Evening Post* in the mail once a week—and so I probably read their article "Is the World Getting Warmer?"

About the time I started high school in 1953, both *Time* magazine and *Popular Mechanics* were running warnings by the infra-red heat expert Gilbert Plass. We also subscribed. But I likely forgot all about the problem because the Cold War and thermonuclear bomb testing seemed much scarier than any drip-drip-drip scenario—one even slower than dry rot from an unrepaired roof leak.

But five years later, when I was a physics major at Northwestern University, there was a weekly film series in the engineering auditorium and one cold Friday night, among the short subjects preceding the main feature, my girlfriend and I saw a short documentary on global warming directed by Frank Capra. (You too can view it[1] via YouTube's archive and marvel at the old "straight man" attempts to provide comic relief; the diagnosis and prognosis were, however, right on.) Then I read Plass' 1959 article in Scientific American, "Carbon Dioxide and Climate."

It must have been consciousness-raising because of what happened ten years after that, at the Scripps Institution of Oceanography at the University of California in San Diego. It has one of the most beautiful settings in the world for doing science, with its long pier out into the Pacific Ocean and its Mediterranean climate. A freshly minted Ph.D. in physiology and biophysics, I was there for a neurobiology meeting when I wandered into the wrong auditorium. It turned out to be a seminar for the oceanographers on the role of the ocean in absorbing the excess CO_2 from fossil fuels.

I remembered that this was an interesting topic and sat down in the back of the room. By that time, I'd had to teach acid-base chemistry to medical students and so I assumed that I could understand the oceanographers.

By happenstance, I was sitting at the very heart of global warming awareness. Though I didn't realize it in 1969, it was the oceanographers at Scripps who started taking global overheating seriously back in the 1950s. (In 1958, they started monthly sampling of mountain-top CO_2 in Hawaii—imagine that, oceanographers working atop Mona Loa, the world's largest volcano!)

That CO_2, even in trace amounts, could trap heat had been known since the experiments of Joseph Fourier in the 1820s—he of math's Fourier Transform, he who accompanied Napoleon to Egypt in 1798, he who served as governor of Lower Egypt for a while.

Later in 1861, the Irish physicist John Tyndall first suggested that global warming from excess CO_2 might be possible.

In 1896, the Swedish physicist Svante Arrhenius presented the results of two years of paper-and-pencil calculations, showing that an anthropogenic doubling of CO_2 concentration could warm up the air by 5°C (9°F). That's close to modern estimates.

This didn't alarm him. Arrhenius quipped that Stockholm might be improved by a little more heat—though it might have been a double entendre. (One must understand that his wife had left him, one of the reasons he spent a lot of long winter evenings alone with pencil and paper, doing long division.) He later won the Nobel Prize in chemistry for other work; he considered his climate work "a hobby."

But in the six decades that followed Arrhenius, each time that someone raised concerns about overusing fossil fuels, there were two standard ways of dismissing the problem. Some physicists would claim that water vapor would mask the effect of excess CO_2. Chemists would say that the oceans were capable of taking up the excess CO_2, buffering it by making more bicarbonates. No CO_2 rise, therefore no overheating—so stop worrying about overusing coal and oil.

Plass repeated Arrhenius' calculations with the most advanced computers of the 1950s and overcame the water vapor objection[2]. He also provided a timeline for the overheating that had been missing before. The Johns Hopkins University physicist predicted that if we kept burning fossil fuels, the amount of CO_2 in the air would double by the year 2080. That's in the range of modern estimates.

About the same time, ocean scientists realized that the oceans couldn't possibly absorb all of the excess CO_2 (the current data shows it has only taken up 25 percent so far—but that's enough to significantly acidify the ocean surface[3]). Roger Revelle, then the head of Scripps, recognized the incomplete absorption of excess CO_2 as a looming public policy problem and worked hard to raise the consciousness of both scientists and policymakers about global warming. In 1964, the U.S. National Academy of Sciences issued a study that recognized the possibility of "inadvertent weather modification" caused by the burning of fossil fuels. But even Revelle thought that really serious climate effects were still centuries into the future.

Projections then simply assumed that the 1950s fossil fuel emissions would continue in the future at the same rate. No allowance was made for population growth and none for increased use by developing countries. Even if they had included such expansion of use, no one back then would have believed that world population could triple in a mere sixty years.

But emissions are instead up five-fold and the feverish future is now arriving faster and faster because the emissions are rising exponentially, not linearly. Emissions of CO_2 grew 1% each year in the 1990s at the time of the 1997 Kyoto Protocol. Instead of growth reversing as it did for the ozone-depleting gases after the 1987 Montreal Protocol, carbon emissions instead soared. Since 2003, annual growth has been 3% globally.

This is more than the most extreme estimates made in the 1990s for future emissions. The same thing happened with projections of sea level rise[4]. And the summer when there is no Arctic sea ice left looks like it is going to happen about forty years sooner than the seemingly reasonable estimates of only a decade ago.

Low-ball estimates are a recurring problem in climate science. They often leave out any part of the mechanism that requires a guess rather than a number from hard-earned data. Economists routinely do the same thing for an economic forecast, leaving out the chance of, say, a housing bubble bursting.

But an insurance company[5] that so underestimated risks would be wiped out. They, at least, cannot afford to leave out those risk factors that are difficult to quantify.

Let me summarize why *emissions reduction* is now an obsolete strategy:

In half of the climate models, global average overheating is more than 2°C by 2048. But in the US, we get there by 2028. Drastic emissions reduction worldwide would only buy the US nine extra years. It is a similar story for other large countries.

Achieving zero emissions globally would still result in severe climate problems for centuries, with one-fourth of the excess CO_2 still in the air a thousand years later.

Given that developing countries are even less likely to control their use of fossil fuels than the developed countries that have failed to do so, we can expect them to continue to burn their own fossil fuels in order to modernize.

We can no longer rely on approaches that require major social engineering or major research breakthroughs. What was reasonable a few decades ago is no longer enough, given the interim CO_2 accumulation and the climate problems that have already appeared.

Emissions reduction does not reduce ocean acidification anytime soon.

Nor does it soon reduce the chance of an abrupt climate shift.

3
The Climate Docs

Even experienced physicians overestimate survival time for two-thirds of their terminal cancer patients[1]. And the better the physician knows the patient, the greater the overestimate of survival time—a clear indication that wishful thinking is biasing the physician's prediction.

Suppose that we have been overestimating the time left before serious societal collapse from climate change? That's surely the prudent assumption to make.

The climate scientists have, after all, been placed in the awkward position of acting as the planet's physicians. However, playing planetary physician is not a job they aspired to or trained for. No mentor provided an example of how to persuade the patient to stop smoking or to do surgery on a damaged lung. No one showed them in the emergency room what to do first when there are closing windows of opportunity.

Nor do climate scientists yet have the mindset of physicians. They haven't been taught, as were the hundred generations of physicians since Hippocrates, that "Life is short, the art long, opportunity fleeting, experience treacherous, judgment difficult. The physician must be ready, not only to do his duty himself, but also to secure the cooperation of the patient, of the attendants, and of externals." Note that secure-the-cooperation bit.

In short, if you are knowledgeable enough to judge that the immediate future is deadly, you have a duty to stage-manage the intervention until someone better trained comes along. It's like your duty, upon spotting a house fire, to phone for help and wake up the inhabitants by pounding on the windows or throwing rocks at them. You have knowledge that they do not. You don't understate the problem, leaving out the scary bits, as some climate scientists tend to do.

Most of us have no body of accumulated wisdom about delays, the way generals and physicians do. "If you wait until you have 100 percent certainty, something bad is going to happen on the battlefield," says General Gordon R. Sullivan, the former Chief of Staff of the U.S. Army.

Unjustified delay in starting treatment has happened often enough in medicine that there is now a cautionary aphorism about postponing treatment while refining the diagnosis: "The doc who waits until dead certain winds up with a dead patient."

The ad hoc climate docs have it even harder than the ER docs. They are encountering not just denial of illness but flacks paid to encourage delay, lately using lies, slander, and less obvious forms of misrepresentation. It's like having a well-paid flack in the emergency room, constantly trying to distract physicians from doing what is in the patient's best interests.

Some climate scientists have been distracted from leadership duties by calls for more and more "certainty." Who isn't in favor of understanding things better? But emphasizing uncertainty is also a technique that is often used by lobbyists to postpone action, promoting the suspension of judgment until another big report comes out five years hence. And then another one in another five years.

There is one bright spot in this sorry story of the emerging climate crisis. It isn't (yet) a classical Greek tragedy in which the main character is brought to ruin because of the extreme consequences of some tragic flaw or weakness of character, with a Greek chorus standing around commenting on his hubris but helpless to intervene.

Unlike the terminal patients, there is nothing inevitable about our civilization's fate under CO_2 poisoning. We could, for example, take the excess CO_2 out of the air, recapturing past emissions—much as renal dialysis now saves patients in kidney failure from their accumulating toxins. It's probably going to require fertilizing one percent of the ocean surface[2] and then sinking the new biomass into the ocean depths before it turns back into CO_2.

We can still back out of the danger zone for most climate leaps, if we reverse fast enough—say, finish the clean-up job in the next twenty years.

Emissions reduction is still as essential as ever. But now we must keep the long term solutions relevant by a quick and massive cleanup of past emissions. Physicians will recognize this as the difference between surgery and an adjuvant treatment such as chemotherapy. It's an adjuvant when it is, by itself, insufficient—but when used after a more effective treatment such as surgery, helps to keep the problem from coming back.

We are now in a situation where emissions reduction per se is clearly insufficient. Even if we somehow stopped all emissions tomorrow, we'd still expect serious climate problems to continue for centuries because our excess CO_2 would remain up in the air.

Risk is the likelihood multiplied by the consequences—and we have already stumbled into the high-risk zone, judging from the abrupt climate shifts that began in 1976.

I'd say that we are facing a medium likelihood of widespread catastrophe within the next few decades, rather like flying on a plane with a 30 percent chance of losing a wing before landing. Even when the "most likely" scenario is that we would arrive safely, we'd strive mightily to avoid flying on that airplane in the first place.

Time's up. It's clear that the planetary emergency has already arrived. Only swift action to recapture past emissions can be an effective treatment.

4
How Much Time Do We Have Left?

"Doc, just how long do I have left? A year?"

If the patient has a gradually failing heart, the physician's lengthy answer might boil down to "One to two years if it's just gradual deterioration. But you could also have a heart attack at any time. Don't count on even three months to get your affairs in order."

Climate scientists similarly warn of an approaching catastrophe by climate creep—though a climate leap may kill off civilization even sooner as the human population crashes.

With business-as-usual emissions producing climate creep, the year of the 2°C fever can be calculated (if you ignore the possibility of climate leaps in the meantime): it's 2048, globally averaged. The United States gets there by 2028. Calculations which take account of the CO_2 and methane released as the Arctic warms and the tundra thaws show we have even less time.

Serious emission reductions delay the 2°C fever by a mere nine years in the US, to 2037. Appallingly, that's all that anyone talks about doing in response to our changing climate—despite the fact that it neither stops making things worse nor rids us of the accumulated past emissions.

There are other ways in which the current climate projections understate the problem we face. First, forecasts for climate creep operate on the assumption that climate change is gradual because CO_2 accumulation is gradual. But that's no longer a fair assumption, and for two separate reasons.

First, the excess CO_2 can bump up quickly. The big 1997 El Niño almost did that. Had its droughts lasted a second year, we could have lost two major rain forests (the Amazon and Southeast Asia) to fire and rot. That would have liberated enough CO_2 to cause a fifty percent jump in the excess CO_2 in only a few years, setting off heat waves and drought worldwide. That's a lot of climate refugees on the move.

Burn locally, crash globally.

In 2005 and 2010, Amazonia was even more flammable than it was in 1997 when global deforestation emissions temporarily tripled. And once we lose this particular rain forest, it doesn't grow back. Plant succession will stay stuck at grass for a long time, recovering very little of the CO_2 that burning and rotting released into the air. We appear to be on the verge of a mass extinction of rain forest species.

Second, even when the CO_2 accumulation remains gradual, the climate takes leaps for other reasons. They have been happening often enough since 1976 that we already have an alarming track record.

The leap mechanism can be as simple as a sudden circulation shift, the air's version of when a spring flood on a meandering river punches through a new channel—and leaves a U-shaped loop of the old river stranded as a new lake.

Furthermore, because global warming has not been uniform, surprise shifts are becoming more likely. The land has been heating up twice as fast as the ocean surface, creating stronger onshore winds that can punch through old barriers. When they discover an easier path, they deliver their ocean moisture somewhere new.

Figure 1

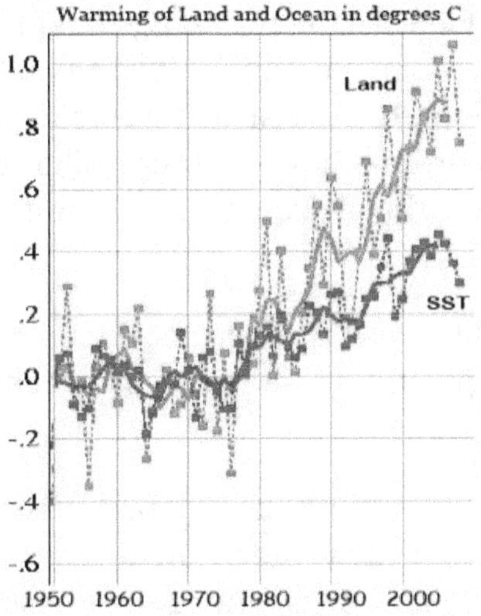

Warming of Land and Ocean in degrees C

Rising land and ocean temperatures. The average land temperature (top) has been rising 2.5X as fast as the sea surface temperature (SST) since 1977. The Arctic (but not the Antarctic) has been warming about four times as fast; as sea ice is lost, more heat is absorbed. Note the relatively flat temperatures from 1950 to 1976. (Solid curves are 5-yr running averages.)

We suppose that the resulting deluge and drought is just "weather" when it happens. It's only when it repeats next year that we begin suspecting a climate leap. Global warming may be the root cause but a global thermometer reading won't necessarily help you understand such rippling effects.

The excess CO_2 has gradually doubled since 1977 and we've seen some climate leaps that are likely due to the overheating produced by CO_2 creep. Most abrupt climate shifts are regional but for brevity I will survey only the leaps since 1976 that became global in extent or implications.

The percentage of land in the two most extreme stages of drought[1] suddenly doubled in 1982. It wasn't just a pulse that comes and then goes. It was a sustained step up, climate change rather than weather. And it wasn't the familiar regional drought. It was many such regional droughts, synchronized around the world.

Global drought stayed that way for fifteen years and then leapt to nearly triple in 1997, stepping back to double in 2005. Millions died.

In addition to those three steps, a persistent rearrangement of winds developed over the winter of 1976–1977 at the termination of a long, large La Niña[2]. Ever since 1982, the warmer El Niños have been large or prolonged and the cooler La Niñas have been small or brief. This is exactly the opposite of the pattern from 1950 to 1976.

Global average temperature, which had been trendless from 1950 to 1976, started ramping up in 1977 at the rate of about 2°C per century. Since about the same year, the jet streams and their storm tracks have been pushed further and further from the equator—as have the subtropical dry bands, thus carrying the Sahara's climate into the Mediterranean. The ramp-like trends in violent weather and forest fires are similar. The trend upwards started even earlier for floods. Climate models[3] show all are to be expected from our global overheating.

Besides four near misses for burning down the Amazon's rain forests, there are signs of instability in the world's best-understood source of abrupt climate change, the circulation shift that lost the Gulf Stream contribution to warming the northernmost Atlantic Ocean.

Northern Europe, at the same distance from the equator as Alaska and Siberia, is warmer and wetter, thanks to a unique mechanism for attracting warm waters into high latitudes. After such waters lose their heat to the winds from Canada, they sink and flow southward in the ocean depths. That makes room for more warm waters to flow into the far north.

But the flushing mechanism, a series of ten-mile-wide whirlpools, is vulnerable. The largest flushing site for the ex-Gulf-Stream waters, in the Greenland Sea north of Iceland, shut down in 1978. It recovered over the next decade. Then the second largest, in the Labrador Sea between southern Greenland and

Canada, shut down in 1997, suddenly recovering over the winter of 2007–2008. It also shut down back in the 1970s.

Were both to shut down together, stopping much of the extra heat export from the tropics into the northernmost Atlantic Ocean, we would expect serious climate change from the wind rearrangements that would follow the sea surface cooling. Europe might not get the quick freeze that such circulation shifts caused several dozen times in the last ice age, but the sudden rainfall shifts would still threaten its agriculture and thus the viability of its big cities.

Thus it appears that world climate has already become highly unstable. In each decade since 1976, we have averaged several leaps and several near misses. That track record—not computer forecasts—is why we need a very fast intervention to head off future climate instabilities.

Climate leaps are like heart attacks, ranging unpredictably from minor to catastrophic—say, a human population crash from war, famine, pestilence, and genocide. It's a very different time scale than for global warming, both sudden and sooner. To ignore the climate leaps so far on the grounds that they haven't caused major catastrophes is like ignoring minor heart attacks.

That means that this is no longer just about our grandchildren's world. Or that of our children. It's about *our* future—even that of today's senior citizens.

We have been fiddling while the Earth burns. Though near-zero emissions are still essential for the long run, the most critical threat has become civilization collapsing in the meantime following a climate leap.

Figure 2

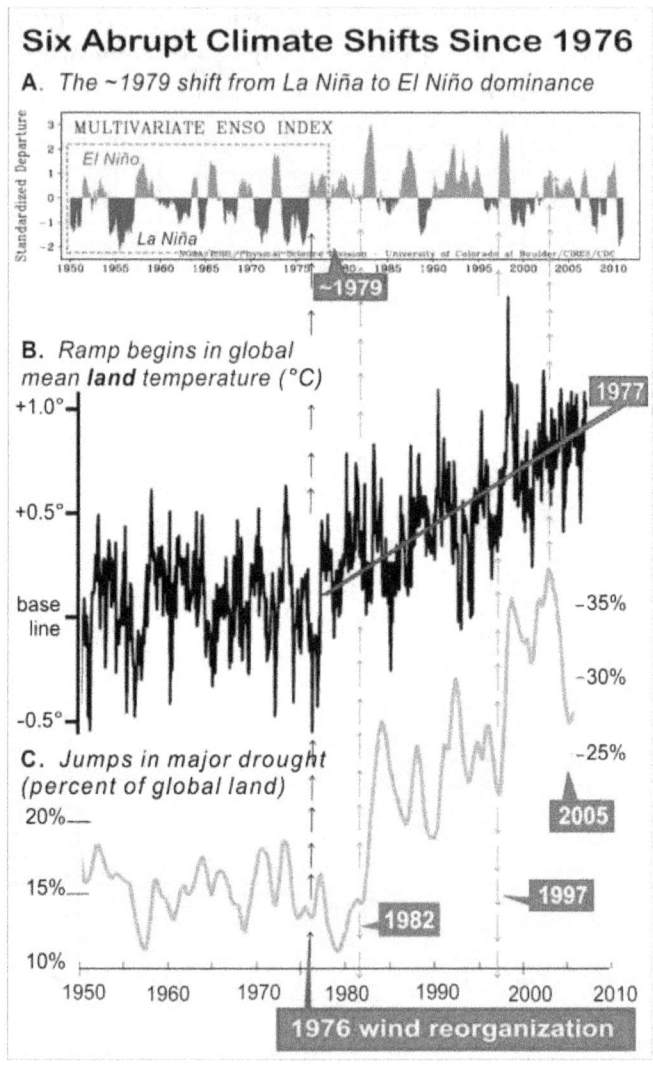

Abrupt Climate Shifts

A. The MEI is an index* that combines the usual central Pacific temperature with western Pacific wind speed and direction, showing much sharper transitions. The 1950–1976 period was dominated by La Niña conditions, some large and long. It was replaced by the current regime dominated by larger and longer El Niño modes sometime between the defining events of 1976 and 1982 (for convenience, ~1979).

B. Global mean temperature on land[4] had no trend between 1950 and 1976, then began ramping up in 1977 at about 0.2°C per decade. A two-month sliding average has been applied; not corrected for volcanic cooling following major eruptions in 1982 and 1991.

C. The fraction of global land surface in major drought (PDSI<-3) stayed near 14% until the large El Niño of 1982. Then it surged to 27%, about double the base. With the large 1997 El Niño, global drought surged to triple, peaking at 37% in 2003. It suddenly dropped back to double in 2005. Adapted[5] from Dai et al 2004 as updated in 2006.

The 1976 reorganization of circulation was first spotted in the western Pacific[6] about the time that the last large and long La Niña ended.

Why the echo? No, you didn't lose track of what page you were on. There really are some sentences that repeat points made in earlier chapters. While some repeats are a teaching strategy, in this book there is an additional reason.

I am trying to craft each chapter so that, in addition to carrying along the main story through the book, any one chapter is sufficiently self-contained to stand alone as an op-ed or feature article, or to be assigned as reading for a course. Or so that you can email a chapter to someone without having to explain what was said in earlier chapters.

PDFs of individual chapters, with citations appended, can be downloaded from _WilliamCalvin.org/media_.

As the copyright page notes, any single chapter may be freely reproduced. No need to ask first, though a brief notification or clipping sent to _WCalvin@UW.edu_ would be appreciated.

5
Underestimating Climate

Forget, for a moment, all of the politicians who deny the major findings of climate science—despite knowing nothing about the subject. Let's focus instead on the knowledgeable policymakers who already "get it."

What do they think the climate problem is all about? Is that exaggerated? Watered down?

What do they think should be done about it—and how quickly?

Do their opinions match up with what climate scientists say?

The standard view seems to be that *fossil fuel emissions are the problem.* Some also understand the causal chain from fossil fuels to CO2, from excess CO2 to overheating, and then to such domino-effect climate problems as the Sahara's climate expanding into southern Europe. *There's no mention of sudden climate shifts in the standard view.*

They think that reducing annual emissions is the proper response. *There's no mention of repairing the current climate in the standard view*; it's simply a future trend that needs long-term corrections.

The average climate scientist would probably agree, though with caveats. However, this framing of the problem and the response does assume (a) that the climate will change slowly as the global temperature slowly ramps up. It assumes (b) that the problem is still in the future. And it assumes (c) that going after the root causes—cutting down forests and burning fossil fuels—is still an adequate strategy for dealing with the problem.

Though true a half-century ago, all three assumptions are no longer true, thanks to the CO_2 that accumulated during the decades of little talk and no action.

We now know that climate can leap as well as creep. Imagine, if you will, driving along a nice flat section of a floating bridge in Seattle, with the roadway seen rising up a mile ahead for a bridge under which boats can transit. Vessels that are too tall can be accommodated by a drawbridge in the flat section of the roadway but this is rare. (Only once in fifty years have I had to wait in line for this bridge to close. You forget that it can open.)

Suddenly, with no warning, a wall of steel pops up in front of your car and you crash into it. That's exactly what happened on 22 December 1989 during the morning commute when a shorted-out switch allowed the drawbridge to suddenly begin opening with no preliminaries. Only one driver died, but it was a bizarre scene.

A climate leap can be just as abrupt and just as fatal. We have already had four near misses for the Amazon rain forests to generate an episode of Burn Locally, Crash Globally.

Secondly, even when the CO_2 rises slowly, the way that climate models assume, climate's response can still be a sudden jump—like the one that suddenly doubled the world's drought acreage in 1982, then went to triple from 1997 to 2005. Welcome to nonlinear systems[1], where two plus two can equal a dozen, surprises are frequent and things suddenly pop up.

Several more global-scale shifts started in 1976—and that's not counting the many regional shifts. The best-studied one was a rearrangement of winds in the western Pacific Ocean tropics, which may well have something to do with changing the El Niño cycle and the end of flat global temperatures despite the rising CO_2. That's also when the deserts began to expand.

So the climate problem is not merely a future one: we have already created dangerous climate instability. Those drought steps were surprises. Climate science has not advanced far enough yet to understand their mechanics, much less predict them with climate models.

A large-enough climate leap could trigger a human population crash. Worse, it might close off the escape route, so that the Earth spirals up into a hothouse that causes a mass extinction of species and thoroughly trashes the planet.

Is the low-carbon energy diet an adequate treatment for such climate disease? Far from it: reduced emissions are unlikely to stop the instability, not for centuries. Nor will it stop rising sea level, expanding deserts, ocean acidification, and the escalating problems with heat waves and forest fires, deluge and drought.

Reducing emissions is like limiting the annual number of trucks allowed into a garbage dump; the height of the pile still grows, just not as fast. Zero emissions is like closing the dump; the pile still remains, only slowly settling somewhat. Getting rid of the truck traffic doesn't make the pile go away.

It's the excess CO_2 already in the air that's become the major climate culprit, not future emissions. The only sensible response is to clean up the CO_2 dump *and* counter any continuing emissions—and to do this before an abrupt climate shift occurs that is big enough to set off a human population crash.

Yet the standard view of the climate problem only looks to delaying future aggravations; it is much like the longer-term treatment of cardiovascular problems with a more appropriate diet.

Even top climate scientists have been saying things like "Techniques for extracting atmospheric CO_2 (like bio-sequestration) might eventually prove necessary," as if there were no real urgency about reburying the fossil CO_2.

It is time to revise this outdated framing to focus on climate instability and a quick cleanup of the excess CO_2. That's like doing an arterial cleanout for the near-term threat of heart attack and stroke—while continuing the cardiac diet. Climate repair buys time so that the longer-term solutions have a chance to work.

Scientists like to focus on the things that they don't know, since that is the cutting edge of scientific research. So they don't keep repeating the things that they do know, which is one reason the public and the media often don't hear from scientists about the strong areas of agreement on global warming.
—Joe Romm, 2008[2]

Scientists have an annoying habit of backing off when they're asked to make a plain statement, and climatologists tend to be worse than most.
—Mark Bowen, 2005[3]

For years now, large numbers of prominent scientists have been warning, with increasing urgency, that if we continue with business as usual, the results will be very bad, perhaps catastrophic. They could be wrong. But if you're going to assert that they are in fact wrong, you have a moral responsibility to approach the topic with high seriousness and an open mind. After all, if the scientists are right, you'll be doing a great deal of damage.

—Paul Krugman, 2011[4]

6
Speaking Too Softly

Alerting the public and policymakers about global overheating has made so little progress since 1950 that we're still trying to get the old message across rather than addressing the new threats from the present-day accumulation of CO_2.

So why have climate scientists settled for such an outdated, inadequate framing of the climate problem?

To some extent, they have to focus on those parts of the problem that the public and policymakers can comprehend. Knowledgeable politicians usually advise them to tailor the message to emphasize clean energy. Unfortunately, history shows that this can lead to further tailoring of the message to what reluctant ears will listen to—say, reporting smoke rather than the fire you observed.

And the psychologists have told them that fear-based appeals, especially those not coupled with a clear solution, can backfire. Telling the climate story, and ending with a list of emissions-reduction possibilities, is more likely to make people believe the underlying science than is an explanation pointing to a catastrophe, with no proposal for avoiding it.[1]

Also, basic scientists are usually not tasked with recommending actions to be taken, the way that engineers are. They see themselves as responsible for exploration and explanation. A few see themselves as neutral arbiters of the facts with a duty not to take sides, should political sides form up.

Scientists can also be prone to understatement for ironic contrast, as in Charles Darwin's only mention of human evolution in his *On the Origin of Species*, "Light will be thrown on the origin of man and his history." And there is much understatement in scientific tradition, some "Just the facts, Ma'am" and a general avoidance of emotional coloring in discussing the implications.

Of course, our nonscientist listeners, unfamiliar with our traditions, may take the lack of jumping up and down as a sign that the matter isn't truly urgent.

There are, of course, many people confused by the climate news. But others are clearly in the climate denial business for fun and profit. Consider the attempts to push scientists into understatement of the looming crisis.

• Most obvious are the *intimidation* attempts. When politicians call for another formal investigation of scientists that a half-dozen prior investigations have cleared, one may be forgiven for suspecting that the primary motive is to encourage other climate scientists to keep their heads down.

- *"Alarmists"* is a smear campaign that similarly attempts to intimidate climate scientists. But unlike true alarmists, there is nothing false or exaggerated about their climate warnings. If anything, they have been understating things and we should mentally double their estimates in the manner we do for low-ball bids.

For example, the data for rising sea level and rising emissions have both turned out to be worse than predicted a decade earlier—indeed, as bad or worse than the most extreme of those earlier estimates.

Still, imagine someone who thought big back in 1950 and projected that annual emissions would increase five-fold in sixty years (which they have), due in part to the world population tripling (which it has). No peer-reviewed journal would have published it. Such a scientist would have been laughed off the stage—and, able to guess as much, would have likely softened the message.

- *Oversimplification.* Indeed, the climate warnings of fifty years ago assumed no change in annual emissions and no population growth—one could make the point about climate dangers without including controversial assumptions. It's a way of saying, "It's at least this bad— and likely worse." Except no one says that, knowing what peer-reviewers will pick on.

And back then, there was still some hope that, while some things make the situation worse, maybe we would discover some silver lining that made it better. There is one: CO2 stimulates some plant growth, but not enough to balance things out. Plants sometimes adopt countermeasures such as lowering circulation of air into a leaf's innards.

Alas, we've since discovered many additional effects that will make things even worse—as when the global-warming droughts reduce the acreage on which such stimulated crops can grow. It's the silver lining that wasn't, though the argument is still trotted out by the climate deniers.

In a 2011 analysis of how much permafrost will melt with further CO_2 accumulation from fossil fuel use[2], the authors omitted the additional overheating that will be caused by the secondary CO_2 and methane released from melted permafrost. Leaving out such vicious cycles is a reasonable cropping of the permafrost problem because including it would have taken them into the more difficult territory of modeling how much of the tundra's carbon will be released as CO_2 and how much as methane (far more effective at overheating the planet).

Scientists familiar with modeling strategies can make allowances for such "It's at least this bad" understatement of a problem—but journalists and lawmakers generally cannot.

• Then there is a heavily promoted notion that scientists' *political views* might cause overstatement of the climate threat. It seems more likely that the assertion of political bias is pernicious misdirection, just another way to make the climate alarm sound like "mere opinion" rather than science—and stirring up "My opinion is just as good as yours" sentiments in the general public.

• Or that it's all a hoax. To quote a 2011 New York Times editorial: 'The Republican presidential contenders regard global warming as a hoax or, at best, underplay its importance. The most vocal denier is Rick Perry, the Texas governor and longtime friend of the oil industry, who insists that climate change is an unproven theory created by *"a substantial number of scientists who have manipulated data so that they will have dollars rolling into their projects."'*

•••

Besides the pressures on climate scientists, there are also psychological traps to consider as we try to understand the prevalence of the soft sell. I would ordinarily hesitate to provide a cognitive roadmap that the climate denial industry could exploit. But by now, it is clear they have already figured out such vulnerabilities for themselves and spent millions of dollars accordingly.

• Like the rest of us, climate scientists tend to *pigeon-hole problems* but they have become very narrowly focused ("overspecialization"). If one is to judge by talks at climate science conferences, climate creep is *the* problem. Climate leap is simply not on the agenda. An abrupt climate shift is seldom mentioned, even in passing, by the speakers.
  And so you hear people talk about fixing emissions as "fixing climate." Even at a conference of climate scientists, no one stands up to correct them by saying, "Wrong. That's

like confusing miles with miles per hour. Zeroing emissions is only going to minimize the rate at which the climate problems worsen. You have to actually remove the excess CO_2 to fix the climate problems."

• It seems prudent to assume that some climate scientists will fall into the same *empathy trap* that physicians do when overestimating how much time a cancer patient has left[3]. Alas, such wishful thinking could be fatal by wasting what little time we have left to repair the climate.

• Among the cognitive factors is the *drill-down psychology.* Most scientists and engineers, if confronted with a problem, first try to drill down through the intermediate layers of cause to the most basic of the underlying ones. It's not unlike a pilot following the well-tested checklist for fuel problems to determine what switch to throw next— except that scientists won't have a checklist or a switch to throw, just good skills for peeling back the layers.

Climate scientists long ago drilled down to fossil fuel emissions as the biggest underlying cause of overheating and thus of the domino effects—and so most think that reducing emissions is the obvious way to go. (And so it was.) But some could now argue that they have become trapped in a paradigm.

• *A long journey begins with a single step* is a cognitive notion that compounds the problem—that we must first stop next year's emissions from becoming 3% larger than this year's, then gradually reduce emissions to zero. That logic puts cleaning up the CO_2 accumulation ("negative emissions") as the very last thing to do.

I've even heard a perverse argument for keeping it in last place: initially, a cleanup project will only be big enough to offset some of the continuing emissions—it sounds like getting credit for planting a few trees. And so some people are against carbon sequestration projects because they want to keep the pressure on the fossil fuel industry, without realizing what the consequences are of delaying a full cleanup.

• *No one likes being the bearer of bad news.* Even though shooting the messenger has gone out of style, a knowledgeable messenger may be asked, "So, what do we do now?" And the messenger, though the most knowledgeable person in the room, doesn't yet have an adequate answer.

So the messenger sticks to the part of the climate problem for which solid numerical estimates can be given, such as how much it will gradually overheat by the end of this century. But that redefines the problem by cropping out the messy parts, the same way that economic forecasts leave out estimates for a bubble bursting, as happened in 2008.

• Then there are *reputations to protect.* In addition to wanting to appear sober and reliable, many of the knowledgeable scientists will recall sectarian warnings of the apocalypse— and their general disrepute (they are standard fare for

New Yorker cartoons). Or of Chicken Little running around shouting, "The sky is falling!"

This could lead some climate scientists to back off from saying anything that could be interpreted as just another instance. To do so, many must reason, would lower one's reputation and thereby one's ability to get across even the standard framing of the climate problem. They could be right.

•Another psychological possibility is that some of the knowledgeable people are in *denial*; it certainly happens to physicians often enough.

That the whole earth could get into big trouble with a mass extinction of species—and that the human population could be drastically downsized by resource wars, starvation, epidemics, and genocides—is a hard concept to digest, a bitter pill indeed when low-tech human activities are so clearly the cause.

• *"The little boy who cried wolf"* also affects the psychology. Researchers in the earth sciences are well aware of the quandary posed by improving methods for predicting the time of a big earthquake. People psychologically adapt to frequent predictions that are unfulfilled, particularly if it involves bundling up the family and joining the traffic jam leading out of town. And so perhaps one should wait until dead sure?

One has to distinguish[4] between *predictions* (something is *likely* to happen *sometime* soon) and *warnings* based on travel time (it's already happened but will take time to get here). Tsunami warnings sometimes provide evacuation lead times of hours. Even a ten-minute earthquake warning is useful for taking cover under something big and heavy and for stopping traffic before it can wander off the road or across the center line.

But predictions are usually probabilistic, even when based on precise data—say, predicting a 50% chance of a big earthquake in the next ten days. But when you go to update the warning a week later, many people will just ignore it. Many climate scientists come out of an academic tradition where this prediction quandary is recognized.

• *"Avoiders"* (a subclass of "inactivists") are aware of the climate threat and accept the science. But they don't want to talk about it because their own ethics would then require them to act—and action would be disruptive to their lives. One hears, for example, of undergraduate courses where, once the climate topics roll around, the students look bored. "They've grown up hearing that the world is going to hell," said a professor, "and they tune out."

There are also cultural traditions of avoidance, as in "Don't speak of the Devil." Until recently, it was standard medical practice in Japan to avoid telling cancer patients about their diagnoses "to protect them from distress."

Sometimes, the postponing style of avoidance becomes integral to a society's decision-making processes. In the immediate aftermath of the one-two punch of the 2011 Japanese earthquake-tsunami, government officials withheld much nuclear reactor data from the public and other governments. "Everything in their system is built to build consensus slowly," said one American official at the time[5]. "And everything in this crisis is about moving quickly." (Sounds like climate, doesn't it?)

• Closely related is the *cop-out*: delaying action because of fearing failure and wanting nothing to do with a failure. This is rather the antithesis of the hero of literary traditions—a person who, though aware of the personal risks, sees a job that must be done for the community's good and promptly plunges in and does it. Medical schools try to prepare physicians to recognize and avoid cop-outs but few scientists or policymakers are similarly familiar with the warning signs of avoidance.

• Almost none of us are trained, in the manner of physicians and generals, to think like a crisis manager in situations when the remaining uncertainties must be balanced against the need for quick action. (I only know it secondhand, thanks to a long association with academic neurosurgeons and psychiatrists.)

Unlike scientists, physicians often deal with *urgent situations*. They are frequently presented with a situation in which multiple things have gone wrong—and more can go wrong in the next hour.

Too many patients have died because someone got so wrapped up in sorting out the diagnostic possibilities that the ABCs were briefly neglected. Five minutes of failing to notice that the heart stopped means that half of such patients cannot be resuscitated. And so there is an ABC checklist for unconscious patients: A is for Airway (gently lifting the chin, tilting the head backward, improves air flow). B is to check for Breathing (watch the lower chest). C is for Circulation (check skin color, feel the pulse).

But for the ad hoc climate docs, it's more like being the pilot of a jumbo jet when an engine has disintegrated, sending shrapnel into the wing and body of the plane— cutting tubes, control wires, and electrical cables. There are no checklists for a pilot in such complex situations— just some priorities such as keeping the plane in the air and putting out the fires.

•••

A human population crash will occur should we fail to act decisively. The global-scale climate instability seen since 1976 says that this catastrophe could happen any year with little warning, not merely later this century.

Fortunately, we are not yet committed to a spiraling greenhouse effect that will trash the globe. There is still something we can do to avoid that hothouse path and repair the global climate. Removing CO_2 from the air can back us out of the danger zone for abrupt climate shifts, back us out of ocean acidification, reverse the expansion of the deserts, reverse perhaps half of the rise in sea level—and cool things off.

We probably still have time to save ourselves—but we are now so far down the road to a climate catastrophe that our climate repair must now be big and quick.

7
Low-Ball Estimates

Why are there so many climate underestimates? Is this just like the chronic problem of cost underestimates for big projects and the subsequent budget overruns?

No. For a number of reasons, it is worse. Estimating future emissions, for example, is just a guess guided by extrapolating some elements of the past. Yet past weather records don't help much when the base state changes, such as when the hundred-year flood starts occurring twice as often. (One then says that the statistics "aren't stationary anymore.") We're increasingly in an "All bets are off" situation where many elements of the past are no longer a good guide.

For example, suppose your home weather station has given you a quarter-century record of peak wind speed—and then your neighbor cuts down a lot of big trees. Suddenly you start seeing much stronger winds than before; those trees had sheltered you. This change in underlying ground-state conditions means that your old wind records are no longer a good indicator of what might happen in the future (and that maybe you should cut down that nice old tree close to the house, now exposed to stronger wind gusts).

Furthermore, projections often leave out anything that is difficult to express as a number, such as the possibility of an economic downturn, a housing bubble bursting, a tightening of credit, or a trade war. When a climate scientist has just devoted a few years to reducing the error bars for one term of the heat balance equation, it is probably distasteful to then include a new term based on a mere guess.

Or maybe something was left out of the analysis. In the immortal words of the U.S. Secretary of Defense, Donald Rumsfeld (who was, in fact, paraphrasing Confucius via Henry David Thoreau), "There are known knowns. (These are things we know that we know). There are known unknowns. (That is to say, there are things that we now know we don't know.) But there are also unknown unknowns. (These are things we do not know we don't know.)"

The famous scientific example is Lord Kelvin's erroneous conclusion in 1862 that our planet could not be as old as Darwin said it was or it would have cooled down a lot more from losing its original heat into space. Good physics for the time, but he didn't know about the abundant heat produced by radioactive decay, discovered in 1903, which heats the earth's surface from within to supplement the sunshine.

Revelle's generation didn't know about abrupt climate change either—and it's what is likely to get us into serious trouble long before the gradual overheating does. No one knew about the ancient climate leaps until 1984, when they were discovered in a Greenland ice core. It appeared that the air temperature over southern Greenland had taken a large step up in just several years. When I heard the Swiss physicist Hans Oeschger report this in a talk he gave in Seattle in 1984, I was astonished that the knowledgeable audience didn't ask very many questions about it.

But, as I should have realized, there were simpler explanations to rule out first, such as missing data. Perhaps a surface melt removed a few centuries of ice before a new layer was added on top—making a gradually changing climate look like a sudden change. Such "unconformities" from missing layers are common enough in layer-cake geology, where a sudden change in rock type is because erosion removed the transition layers. I'd seen many big unconformities where they are exposed in the bottom of the Grand Canyon[1].

Figure 3

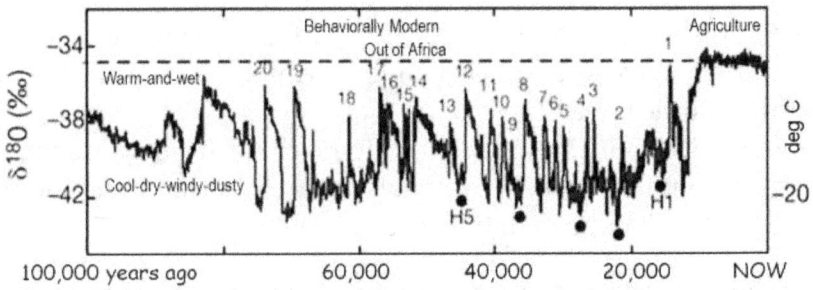

Abrupt climate shifts during the last ice age and what humans were doing at the same time. Note the chattering just before 50,000 years ago. GRIP ice core records from the summit of Greenland, where changes in the concentration of oxygen-18 serve as a proxy for air temperature near Greenland. Adapted from William H. Calvin, *A Brain for All Seasons: Human Evolution and Abrupt Climate Change* (University of Chicago Press 2002).

Ruling out unconformities was one motivation for drilling at the summit of Greenland in the early 1990s, where it is high enough and cold enough so that summer sunshine never thaws the surface snow. Drilling down to bedrock through the accumulated ice gave the climate scientists a "two-mile time machine" that took climate records back to the prior warm period in the ice ages, about 120,000 years ago[2].

There were over forty abrupt events during the most recent glaciation: half were steps into the cold, half were sudden rewarmings—some almost up to modern temperatures. Sometimes, such as between 55,000 and 50,000 years ago, temperatures chattered back and forth between a warm-and-wet climate and a cool-dry-windy-dusty climate, pausing for only a few centuries at one extreme or the other before flipping back[3].

When most climate scientists hear "abrupt climate change," they think of those Dansgaard-Oeschger flips seen in the ice cores. And, because there isn't enough winter pack ice in the North Atlantic Ocean these days, those who know something about sea ice contributions to the flip mechanisms may assume that, without the dramatic reversals in surface brightness, such a quick flip can't happen in the near future.

The modern sudden climate shifts, beginning in 1976, aren't quite as dramatic. But because civilization is so overextended— half of us now live in big cities at the end of a long supply line— the result of a modern abrupt shift could be catastrophic even if much smaller.

Having heard dozens of them, and given a few myself, I can report that there is a standard wrap-up for an otherwise scary climate talk that is given by an expert to a general university audience. Whether glaciologist or drought expert, the speaker makes it clear in conclusion that we must clean up emissions, often giving an example of a favorite technology, complete with cautions. ("It's not really 'Clean Coal' unless *all* of its CO_2 is captured and buried.")

Optionally, there's a mention of the value of inventing the new technology ourselves so that exporting it will help solve the balance-of-payments problem.

Almost no one mentions a time scale for recovery, and even fewer mention the danger of abrupt climate shifts in the meantime.

While no one claims that emissions reduction will actually solve our climate problems, this is often inferred by the audience. So this standard summary really constitutes another low-ball estimate—but why?

The climate scientist is likely aware that the numbers don't add up—that even with zero emissions tomorrow, we're still in big trouble—but has nothing constructive to say about a CO_2 cleanup at present. The scientist may well think that no sequestration method is really ripe yet, that they are all too novel or problematic to be mentioned.

But novelty is an evolving thing. No one ever stands up and cheers when a new idea is introduced. Indeed, there's an academic joke about the three stages in the acceptance of a new idea: 1. "It's impossible." 2. "Though possible, it's unimportant." 3. The dismissive "Everybody knows that."

Presented with something novel and thinking as scientists, we usually kick the tires, peel back the layers of the argument and poke them, reserve judgment, and then call for more data and even better understanding. Dissatisfaction is normal.

Then there is tradition. In both science and medicine, summaries are seldom presented as scary. It would be considered "preaching to the choir" as it is assumed that knowledgeable readers can infer the scary aspect for themselves. Indeed, a patient who happened to read his discharge summary, dictated when he was leaving the hospital, might be unable to infer that he was now considered a terminal patient, as the summary was written solely for the knowledgeable.

Readers of the executive summaries of climate reports are often not knowledgeable and, if the scary aspect is not summarized too, they will miss it. Even if they suspect we're now in a scary situation, readers may take the lack of strong emphasis to mean that it's merely a trend that needs correcting over the long run.

Hammering home the message might be more effective than a soft sell.

8
Raising an Uncertain Alarm

If climate scientists have a failing, it's that they hate to sound "alarmist." The deniers and delayers have played on this, just as they have tried to put climate scientists on the defensive by playing on their traditional concerns with accuracy and assignment of cause.

Even a group of distinguished climate scientists, who all believe that climate change is real and menacing, can be hard to keep on topic when abrupt change is introduced into the conversation. They can think about gradual change but few have the tools to approach stepwise change. Any conversation about sudden shifts will quickly transition to "How can we be sure?" complete with all of the multiple-causes hedging that policymakers choose to interpret as a good reason to put off action and send it back for more study.

Some of the emphasis on more approachable problems is necessary to train graduate students and get research grants. In any event, it represents the traditional way in which science makes progress, by defining the frontier between the understood and the unknown. And then chipping away at it.

Engineers may think that science is almost as certain as mathematics. But once you become a graduate student in science, it seems to be all about resolving uncertainty and avoiding premature conclusions. You have to pose questions in a way that forces nature to give you an unambiguous answer.

Crisis management, with its tradeoffs between better understanding and the window of opportunity for effective action, is rarely part of our training. Since there is only one habitable Earth to lose, our thinking about the climate crisis needs to be closer to the physician's focus on a single individual with only one life to lose.

Because of their training, physicians are more likely to see the "certainty" emphasis in climate diagnosis as a cop out, mentally deflecting action, usually from fear of failure. For physicians[1], "Uncertainty is the water we swim in" and the clock is always ticking.

We have also been slow to treat: those who understand the climate threat have been unsuccessful in the Hippocratic "securing the cooperation...of the attendants and of externals" for a variety of reasons ranging from individual denial to the impersonal tragedy of the commons, compounded by paid obfuscation campaigns with budgets far outside the range that nongovernmental supporters of science might be able to fund.

But with knowledge comes responsibility. Let me illustrate this with two safety campaigns of a half-century ago to require the use of seat belts and motorcycle helmets. I remember it well because a girl that I'd once had a crush on was killed when a car overturned and she was thrown out.

The devastating consequences of being thrown out of the car, or into the windshield, was so familiar to physicians that medical groups undertook its prevention with seat belts in the same way that dentists of that era undertook fluoridation campaigns (despite their anticipated loss of income). Most people just didn't know the data. Those who did had a responsibility to the public.

The physicians finally got lawmakers to require that automobile manufacturers include well-anchored seat belts. In the US, it took another forty years before widespread use was achieved. We cannot afford that kind of delay for our climate crisis.

In the case of the motorcyclists' head injuries, and the fate of those who did and didn't wear helmets, it was primarily the neurologists and neurosurgeons who knew about it. In the 1960s, about the time I joined the faculty of our neurosurgery department as a neurophysiology researcher, they undertook to educate the rest of the medical profession about it and to promote laws requiring motorcyclists to wear their helmets.

With specialized knowledge about climate comes the responsibility to act to head off trouble. Many climate scientists have stepped up to the plate over the last fifty years, trying to get those with the power to act to start moving.

9
Core Values and Climate Roulette

While singing in the choir in my youth, I must have listened to several hundred value-laden sermons without ever hearing the phrase "core values." Back then, they were a Boy Scout sort of thing. (They have more recently ruined the iconic "Trustworthy, loyal, and brave" by tacking on clean, reverent, obedient, patriotic, and a laundry list of others.)

Curious about the modern usage, I googled "core values" and up popped service, integrity, quality, diversity, shared purpose, and stewardship of resources.

Dissatisfied with all the mission-statement boilerplate, I asked around at the local espresso café for some examples of values. Ethical behavior. Economic prosperity. Empathy and giving. Fairness. Protection from predators. Respect for tradition. Tolerance and civility. A safety net for the unfortunate. Conservation. Opportunity for all. Government respectful of the people. And one vote for Rock 'n' Roll as a core value.

Valued, certainly, but what rates as a *core* value? Maybe, I mused, it's a value which, if it collapsed, would take the ordinary values down with it. So I tried that on for size. Alas, values don't stack very well.

Later, however, it dawned on me that a stable environment should have been on that list of values—because an unstable climate can undercut most of the other values, leading to their collapse. Losing this type of core value could herald a quick trip back to a time when most lives were "solitary, poor, nasty, brutish, and short."

There is much mention of 'stabilizing' as we talk about global warming and what to do about it. But little of the talk is really about retrieving our previously stable climate.

Most talk of stabilizing simply refers to keeping yearly emissions from further increasing. Imagine a smoker whose pack-a-day habit had gone up to two packs and then three. He could then claim that he had "stabilized" at three because he hadn't progressed to four packs a day. Yet for many people, that's the goal which is supposed to fix climate. And some of them are trying to postpone any action.

The words *instability* and *unstable* have very different climate connotations than does the leveling-off connotation of *stabilizing*. They refer instead to the whiplash shakes that herald an impending collapse, the shaky ladder that prompts you to climb back down and fix its footing.

A changing environment is not necessarily an unstable one. Pure climate creep, featuring the gradual rise in sea level and the northerly waltz of the palm trees, might conceivably occur without the shakes that flirt with collapse.

But our climate dance feels more like the interwoven melodies of Rock 'n' Roll than a waltz, requiring those gyrations that you need to stay upright on a sailboat when the bow rocks up and down while the deck rolls from side to side in a different rhythm. Your body posture has to produce the exact counter melodies for both rhythms or, like Humpty Dumpty, you will take a great fall. (Suppose the Beatles had a boat big enough to dance on?)

Serious instability—the kind that threatens to sink your ship—is more like Leap 'n' Lurch. And for climate, I don't just mean bad regional stuff like Deluge 'n' Drought. Rather it's when Leap 'n' Lurch happens on all continents in the same year, threatening to collapse our civilization via thoroughly disrupting food production and its transport to the big cities.

And while we might see climate's Big Wave coming, being suddenly blindsided is far more likely. A quick punch out of nowhere can occur when the planet runs a fever. What's worse is that the climate punch may not end. It's the punch that never stops giving—knocked down *and* sat upon.

Gradual provocation can result in a sudden shift, as if a switch had been finally been tripped and snapped into a new position. Just recall 1982 when drought suddenly doubled, worldwide. And it stayed up at double—except when it went to triple between 1997 and 2005.

If climate creep is like a slow-motion train wreck, then climate leap is like a heart attack. It comes as a surprise and, since you don't know in advance if it will be minor or catastrophic, the imperative is to prevent it.

All we seem to talk about, however, is climate creep and coping with it—even more slowly. As those drought steps show, that is a totally inadequate framing of our climate problem and of the task facing us.

Our current climate response is mostly a re-emphasis of the old virtues—clean air, clean energy, sustainable agriculture, reforestation, better efficiency, less waste, longer-term thinking—everything that might have kept us from painting ourselves into this corner, had we done them fifty years ago. All are still worth doing, but they do not get us out of the shrinking corner in time.

Our biggest problem is no longer future emissions. It is the excess CO_2 we already have. Now we need an emergency draw down that will make the long-term solutions relevant again.

It's that other virtue which we teach our children as early as possible: Clean up your own mess.

10
Climate Surprises Since 1976

So what are the chances of a climate surprise on a global scale? Is it like a once-a-century flood? Or the fifty-year flood? Maybe one year in every three?

Individually, of course, a surprise is unexpected. If you could forecast it, it wouldn't be a surprise. While we can't forecast leaps yet, we do have a track record to learn from. We can therefore ask: Just how often have we already been blindsided by a global-scale climate surprise? And the answer is one year in every six (if you include the near misses, it's one year in three). We are indeed sitting on a time bomb.

In retrospect, there was a reorganization of Pacific Ocean winds in the winter of 1976-1977 with world-wide climate consequences[1]. You are probably familiar with the tendency of a river to change course when a big flood cuts a new channel, leaving behind oxbow lakes in the old meanders. Or with the way that thoughtless hikers shortcut the switchbacks as they race downhill, creating an express path for runoff to erode the hillside during the next spring melt.

The winds[2] also have faster-flowing "rivers" and, when temperatures rise more in some places than others, such flows can discover shortcuts to their usual paths—and so the winds and waves switch direction and the rain falls somewhere else. It's a special two-for-one deal: Deluge 'n' Drought. In places where soil moisture runs out in mid-summer, there is no more evaporative cooling, boosting land temperature into heat wave territory.

Such a path-switching scenario shows why climate change can be sudden. In less than a year, we can be in big trouble. In other cases, as when effects are cumulative, the time that they began is seen only in retrospect.

From 1950 to 1976, global-average temperature did not have an upwards trend even though emissions tripled[3]. You can imagine the consternation that this caused, how it must have frustrated the work of Roger Revelle and others to get changes in public policy. Contrary to theory, it wasn't warming!

Starting about 1977, however, the land temperature began to ramp up at a rate of 0.2°C per decade—but it took until the 1980s before the trend became convincing. Now, with the perspective of three more decades, the ramp is unequivocal. The only question is whether it is rising exponentially[4], as the CO_2 concentration is doing, or whether it is really linear.

There is still no accepted explanation for the trendless decades. But in control systems engineering, a standard example for plateau-then-ramp behavior comes from the finite capacity of air-conditioning machinery. A human produces more heat than a hundred-watt light bulb. In an auditorium, as the arriving crowd grows past the capacity of the air conditioning to take away their body heat, the air temperature will transition from a plateau temperature (held flat by the thermostat) to a ramp up (as the heat from additional arrivals exceeds cooling capacity).

Figure 4

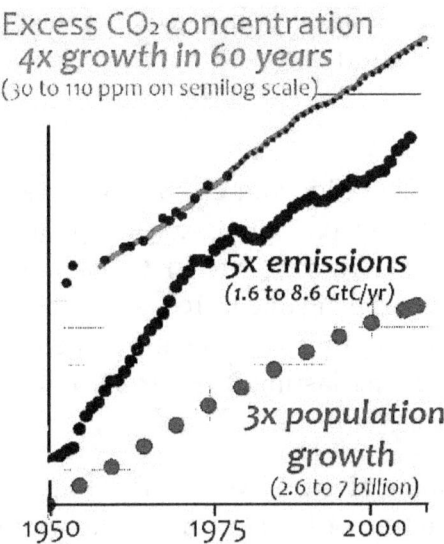

Excess CO_2 concentration
4x growth in 60 years
(30 to 110 ppm on semilog scale)

5x emissions
(1.6 to 8.6 GtC/yr)

3x population
growth
(2.6 to 7 billion)

1950   1975   2000

Excess CO2 and its causes. This is a semilog plot that shows an exponential rise as a straight line. For example, it would show the value of a savings account with compounding interest as a straight line that changes slope when the interest rate changes.

Top: The excess CO2 is rising exponentially. In sixty years, it rose 3.7x.

Middle: The yearly additions of CO2 from fossil fuels ("emissions") grew exponentially until 1973 when Europe and California began working hard to reduce their contributions, slowing the rise. But after 2002, the rate tripled. Overall, it rose 5.3x in sixty years.

Bottom: The world's population rose 2.7X in that period. Source: NOAA.gov.

So it's as if a Gaia-sized thermostat was still capable, before 1977, of handling the incipient overheating with, say, more evaporative cooling or reflective cloud cover. Both could result from ocean overheating serving to put more water vapor into circulation. (Whether this is a sufficient explanation is not established and the cloud response itself is a huge unsettled question dating back to 1927.)

The meta pattern of El Niño and La Niña occurrence underwent a big shift about 1979 as well[5]. Large or lengthy La Niñas had dominated the record from 1950 to 1976, that period of trendless temperatures. Since the big one in 1973-1976, La Niñas have been small (2011 is the exception) or brief and some El Niños became big (1982, 1997) or long-lasting (1987-1988, 1990-1995, and 2002-2005).

The other climate-shifting event of 1976, mentioned earlier, involved the winds and ocean currents of the western Pacific Ocean. Whether this is a cause or consequence of the other shifts cannot be said. So you are free to count the abrupt climate shifts of the 1970s as one, two, or three shifts.

Another three shifts involve the afore-mentioned global drought[6]. There, the shift is immediately felt but you don't yet have the perspective needed to see that it's a decade-scale climate shift rather than the usual ups and downs of annual weather.

From 1950 to 1982, only one acre in every seven was in severe drought at any one time. (That's ignoring the icy acres in Greenland and Antarctica.) Like the land temperature until 1977, there was no upward trend in drought before 1982.

When global drought suddenly doubled in acreage during the big 1982-1983 El Niño, it wasn't just a new peak. Global drought never returned to the old baseline despite a series of La Niñas, staying up near one acre in four.

Then with the next big El Niño in 1997-1998, global drought took another big step up and, despite the La Niña that followed, it stayed up near one acre in every three until suddenly dropping back a notch in 2005—the third stepwise change.

The good news is that the 37 percent drought peak in 2003 didn't trigger a global-scale collapse. However, 70,000 Europeans died in a regional heat wave[7] that same year—even though the globally-averaged temperature did not spike. Cooler temperatures elsewhere in 2003 were of no help to the prostrated Europeans. It's not changing averages (such as global mean temperature) that directly do the damage. It's those record regional extremes and how often new records are set.

So some abrupt climate shifts are seen as steps (1976 wind rearrangement; ~1979 El Niño regime shift; 1982, 1997, 2005 drought steps) and some as ramps (1977ff land temperatures, desert and jet stream moves to higher latitudes, and the trends in wildfires and deluge). And some big associated events are brief pulses (the oversized 13-month-long El Niños of 1982 and 1997). None of this is sorted out yet[8].

The important thing may often be an underlying change of circulation, when the mechanics start working differently and prior statistics no longer apply. When, as the baseball announcers of my youth liked to say when reporting a home run with bases loaded, "Wow! It's now a whole new ball game!"

11
Figuring the Odds

How close have we come to triggering a global disaster? No one knows but it is easy to see how domino effects from even a regional drought could kick global climate deterioration into high gear. Recall Wall Street's "Overreach locally, crash globally" debacle in 2008? A "burn locally, crash globally" scenario is worse.

Indeed, had the record-sized 1997 El Niño lasted twice as long, we could have lost two major rain forests to fire and rot, complete with a mass extinction of species. It only lasted thirteen months (as did 1982's El Niño). Yet some El Niños (say, 1990-1995) have lasted much longer. So far, we haven't experienced a big El Niño that lasted two years.

After three years of a smaller El Niño, a tropical heat wave in 2005—the same one that set up Hurricane Katrina to devastate New Orleans—produced even worse fire danger in the Amazon. Worse than that one was the fire danger from the brief El Niño of 2007. Then, as a modest El Niño ended in 2010, fire danger set another new record.

Had any one of those El Niño droughts lasted twice as long, the resulting surge in CO_2 from burning and rotting could have triggered heat waves on all continents. (Where ever the source,

CO_2 mixes worldwide in several years, what makes the air a global commons.)

The North Atlantic Ocean's overturning circulation—those ten-mile-wide whirlpools that sink surface waters into the depths, described with poetic license in the old Norse sagas—failed more than two dozen times back before agriculture, causing whiplash climate shifts as tropical heat was no longer exported to high northern latitudes. Because evaporation leaves behind so much salt in the chilled surface waters that they become heavy enough to sink through the water below, whirlpools form that can reach far into the ocean depths.

There are predictions of a slow decline of this overturning current. Anything that dilutes the surface water (extra rainfall or melting ice) can stop the flushing—and thus stop the current that brings the extra tropical warmth to the far north. The overturning current could slow by 30 percent in the coming decades in response to global warming's increased rainfall at high latitudes, which dilutes the surface of the ocean[1] and thus shuts down some whirlpools.

Some have thought that the modeling result showing the slow decline was good news, concluding that sudden stoppages were not going to hit us. Alas, the already-observed reality is not as encouraging. The major sinking site, located off northeast Greenland, failed in 1978, recovering during the 1980s[2]. The second largest whirlpool factory is off southwest Greenland in the Labrador Sea. It shut down[3] in 1997, recovering[4] only in the winter of 2007–2008.

Since neither partial shutdown produced a catastrophe, perhaps we have the equivalent of an emergency backup generator. However, nothing prevents both critical sites from failing at the same time—and no one is asking about how to jump-start those whirlpools when they fail.

That's a dozen abrupt climate shifts or near-misses in only 36 years, some of them cliff-hangers for triggering a worst-case scenario. That suggests that the chance of another surprise or near miss next year is about one in three.

Would you fly if there was a one-in-three chance of experiencing an in-flight emergency sometime next year? And that may be an underestimate because the major cause, anthropogenic CO_2 accumulation, has doubled since the 1976 shifts.

What are your lifetime chances of actively participating in the worst-case, death-spiral climate scenario? That's harder to say but the younger you are, the longer your life expectancy—and thus the greater your chance of being around at the wrong time. But even today's seniors may live long enough to see the collapse of civilization.

A one-in-three chance of, say, your country being invaded next year would normally cause an all-hands-on-deck response similar to the mobilizations that preceded World War II. For our political leaders to do nothing but talk would be considered irresponsible and unpatriotic—and to do nothing, unthinkable.

So what are we doing to fix the climate, and back ourselves out of the danger zone for this worst-case scenario? At present, almost nothing. Even for the token response, emissions reduction, it's mostly talk rather than action.

Has Aum Shinrikyo ("Supreme Truth," the wealthy cult obsessed with the apocalypse that hoped to trigger doomsday with its 1995 chemical warfare attacks on the Tokyo subway) found a new way to achieve their goals?

Probably not. But the point remains: the current cast of science-deaf characters (media, lobbyists, politicians) may produce the same result without being fans of the apocalypse. All it takes is being a fan of the status quo. Or of financially starving the government, becoming an anarchist in all but name.

In retrospect, we already have a seriously unstable climate— and we are playing Russian roulette with it.

12
Is "Stabilizing" False Advertising?

Doing now for emissions what we should have been doing fifty years ago ignores all of the anthropogenic CO_2 that accumulated in the meantime, the major cause of those six global-scale climate surprises since 1976.

Because of that, emissions reduction now resembles locking the barn door after the horse is gone—worthwhile, but not exactly recovery either.

This locking-the-barn-afterwards response is often motivated by the politicians' need to be seen "doing something about it." But even such a token response to climate risks has been headed off via denial and delay tactics, patterned on the tobacco industry's forty-year success at buying time by creating confusion over health risks. It is no accident that sowing confusion is better known as "blowing smoke" than as obfuscation.

Even though we can see the fast track to climate disaster, no one even talks about a fast track for cleaning up the mess. Repairing an unstable climate is not what the otherwise excellent climate models and action proposals are all about. They are mostly focused on climate creep and how to slow it down.

Though emissions reduction is advertised as a destination, it is really one milepost on one rather slow road where roadblocks may be frequent and bandits may lurk. In such a situation, wise travelers try to fly instead.

You might have supposed that we were working on climate stabilization because, when scientists speak, "climate" and "stabilizing" often appear in the same sentence. The media may then make the mistake of shortening it to "stabilizing climate."

However, as I mentioned a few chapters back, there are two different meanings of "stabilizing" in play here and some people are hoping that you will confuse them.

1. Stabilizing can refer to flattening a trend, a leveling off— but achieving it is *not* stability in the imperturbable meaning of the word.

2. Stabilizing more commonly refers to preventing collapse, as when we shore up a damaged building, put a walking cast on an injured leg, or otherwise stiffen up something that has become shaky, threatening to collapse. It's what the ER docs mean by "stabilizing the patient's condition," not leveling off at half dead. This kind of stabilizing is proactive, making sure that something doesn't rock the boat.

Unfortunately, leveling off is all that the climate scientists and policy wonks usually mean by stabilizing. Their great fear is that leveling off will be only be achieved when civilization is already half dead.

Note that stabilized does not mean safe—which is often inferred. Furthermore, using the scientific-sounding term *stabilizing,* instead of the more common phrase *leveling off,* may raise false hopes as well as confusion. It matters because a mere leveling off will not achieve climate stability, that happy condition when the climate doesn't wobble and the odds of a really big leap next year returns to the pre-1750 odds of about one in 8,000.

"Stabilizing emissions" merely means stopping the 3 percent annual *increase* in the amount of fossil fuels we burn each year, dumping their CO_2 into the air for free. That's like limiting the yearly number of truckloads allowed in to the garbage dump. Continuing to dump fossil CO_2 into the air, merely at a constant rate, is certainly not going to stabilize climate—in either sense of the word.

More commonly heard is "stabilizing CO_2 levels"—say, leveling off at twice[1] the 280 ppm preindustrial concentration (parts per million; 280 molecules of CO_2 within a million molecules of air.) Leveling off, whether at triple or at today's concentration, requires *zero* emissions, not just reductions. It's like *closing* that garbage dump. But the troublesome pile remains (though settling some over the years).

Still, suppose that we quickly succeed and that the CO_2 concentration levels off. Alas, the excess Deluge 'n' Drought would continue, as would sea level rise. We would not start cooling for another century and even a thousand years out, about one molecule in every four of the excess CO_2 will remain up in the air. Much of any improvement would be due to the ocean absorbing the excess, increasing ocean acidity. And we would still have an unstable climate that spins off surprises—probably even more often than one year in every three.

What will be effective against global-scale Leap 'n' Lurch? It's not just a matter of permanently closing the aerial garbage dump for CO_2. We're going to have to clean up that dump, burying it deeply.

This obvious course for heading off trouble is analogous to drawing down a reservoir, done when an earthen dam is being undermined by a leak, threatening sudden collapse and a devastating flood. There are currently two dams near Seattle where emergency drawdowns had to be done. There is one in California that is threatening Bakersfield with a devastating flash flood.

A long-term solution, such as building a new dam downstream, is not a substitute for a quick fix such as lowering the level of the lake behind the dam. Nor is quickly taking the anthropogenic CO_2 out of circulation a substitute for the low-carbon energy diet needed to prevent the recurrence of climate disease.

Most climate surprises could probably be avoided by quickly cleaning up the excess CO_2 and cooling things off. Taking past emissions out of circulation would lower the global fever, minimize Deluge 'n' Drought, and reverse the ocean's acidification and thermal expansion.

But, given how frequently climate surprises have been occurring, even a twenty year cleanup period might include six surprises. Some might be cliffhangers like 1998, 2005, 2007 and 2010 in the Amazon. One might be big enough to close off our escape route, so that we spiral up to catastrophic climate change.

Our quick fix needs to be really quick. A slow response could be as fatal as when armies mass on the border threatening a blitzkrieg.

That's the what, why, and when of our climate problem. How and where to draw down the CO_2 accumulation is a longer story (my next book, *The Great CO_2 Cleanup*) involving considerations such as big, quick, and secure—and how to avoid undesirable side effects.

What stands in the way of even the locking-the-barn-door minimum, emissions reduction, is an engineered form of political paralysis. The alarmed scientists of the last sixty years have been no match for the proponents of business as usual, with their legions of lobbyists and large advertising budgets locking us in to the greatest tragedy of the commons of all time.

The climate scientists are beginning to feel like Cassandra, the truth-teller in Homer's *Odyssey* who was never believed— even when pointing at the Trojan Horse.

13
The Education of a Climate Consultant

After a long hard day in the boardroom, the old hands among the consultants were trying to cheer up the new climate consultant. Who, despite his second martini, was sinking ever more deeply into despair.

"Try to understand where they're coming from, ClimateGuy," said EconomicsGuy. "All of those vice presidents don't take the long view because, in effect, they are paid not to. That is to say, they are paid to perform superbly in the short run and increase the dividend next year."

"And they can't afford to take the long view," added MarketingGuy. "If they capture the CO_2 from their smokestacks and their competitors don't, their higher price will lose them market share."

"Right," added PoliticsGuy. "They will even tell you that their Board of Directors forces them to be that way—that directors have been sued in the past by shareholders for taking actions that could be predicted to lose market share."

"Furthermore, they think that it's someone else's' job to look out for the long run or the public interest—presumably the government's," said MarketingGuy. "They think that their job is to do everything that isn't actually illegal to maximize their profits. And anti-trust rules keep them from agreeing among themselves to all install new CO_2-capture technology at the same time."

"Excuses, excuses," replies ClimateGuy, morosely. "I was really expecting better from the oil guys. I've met lots of them in small brainstorming sessions and I know that they have to take the long view far more often than industry in general. That's because they have to make an enormous investment in drilling and pipelines for maybe fifteen years before they ever get a revenue stream flowing. And so they give a lot of thought to the trends, to what the market for petroleum products might be twenty years ahead when they have to pay back the borrowed money."

"Yes, but that's also what makes them so resistant to rocking the boat," noted EconomicsGuy.

"How's that?"

"Because they had to make a business plan that laid out, in the prospectus for the bonds they used to finance the drilling project, just what the payback schedule would be like. How much they expect to pump out of the ground. What price they expect to get for it. Just how much of a market decline would cause them to default on the bond interest—or even on the return of principal."

"So?"

"So anything which threatens the continuing execution of that old business plan—say, an electric car—tends to be viewed as something worth delaying for a while," EconomicsGuy said. "And when you stood up in there and told them that all fossil fuel use must be reduced—well, that set off a lot more alarm bells than just those for an electric car. Big Coal gets anxious. So do the railroads that haul the coal cross-country."

"Even if they think you are likely correct about climate," MarketingGuy observed, "they will hope that retrenchment doesn't happen on their shift—not until their kids are through college *and* their own retirement funded. They're not evil people. They're just trapped. They want to delay, not avoid."

"I don't buy that," says ClimateGuy. "This isn't just sins of omission. They're proactive, spending hundreds of millions of dollars on blowing smoke, trying to persuade people that the climate science is uncertain[1], that we can wait until the science is all settled down before doing anything expensive. It's straight out of the tobacco playbook, as are those full-page greenwashing ads."

"Don't forget that little ploy bought the tobacco folks fifty more years of continuing profits," said PoliticsGuy, "a lesson not lost on Big Oil and Big Coal."

EconomicsGuy added, "And the same tactics of science denial were used by groups that deny that HIV causes AIDS, by those who deny evolution, even those who denied the harmful health effects of asbestos[2]. Deniers use a wide variety of deceptive rhetorical tricks that go back to the ancient Greeks. The so-called climate 'debate' isn't a scientific one. It's pretty lopsided, with scientists using scientific evidence on one side, versus paid activists on the other using knee-jerk imagery and rhetorical misdirection."

"The improvement on the tobacco playbook that I've noticed," MarketingGuy volunteered, "is in the uncertainty ploy. Tobacco played the 'doctors are still uncertain' theme song for thirty years. But the fossilfuelers have even gotten the climate scientists to say it for them. Scientists can't open their mouths these days without a little homily about how 'Science is never certain.'"

"I know, I know," replied ClimateGuy. "I wish they would save it for the classroom rather than trying to educate the public about science-in-general at the same time as raising an alarm. It dilutes the urgency of the message."

"Even if they skipped the footnotes, your friends, they'd still be vulnerable to the 'cause-and-effect' ploy," observed PoliticsGuy. "Just look at how often they themselves promote 'single cause' reasoning."

"I catch myself doing that one," said ClimateGuy, "saying 'We can't be sure that the present hurricane is due to global warming.' As if a little lesson in probability theory was always appropriate."

"So if I asked you about the cause of Hurricane Katrina in 2005, what would you say instead?"

"I'd say very forcefully that Katrina is exactly the kind of thing we can expect more of, thanks to global warming. Extreme weather like that is what climate science has been predicting for decades, and now it has arrived—but you'll seldom hear that correct prediction acknowledged on a newscast." ClimateGuy replied.

He continued, "It's silly to talk about '*the* cause' of most events, as if there were only one cause. Everything in the real world has multiple causes acting in combination. And for this hurricane, global warming is very high on the list of big causes. Without the overheating, this kind of event would be rare. And there's nothing uncertain about it."

"The deniers' other big innovation is in framing the issue," observed MarketingGuy. "Especially in using framing for misdirection, for changing the subject. Even some physicists are now going around saying that everything is overblown because the temperature measurements aren't as accurate as they should be."

"Right, as if nature's thermometers like melting ice could be ignored" ClimateGuy said. "First we laid out the logical chain of fossil fuels to CO_2, excess CO_2 to overheating, overheating to climate change. But to hear those blockheads tell it, you're supposed to think that all of the climate effects we've seen since 1976 don't really count if temperature measurement hasn't become as settled as the periodic table of elements. They not only fail to mention nature's thermometers but fail to mention that most of the observed climate changes were predicted long ago by the thermodynamics and the computer models of climate. Only the abrupt climate shifts after 1976, and that temperature-sensitive northward drift of the tropical ring of heavy rain, have been science surprises."

"The hardest thing that I had to get used to in this consulting business,' EconomicsGuy offered, cradling his renewed double scotch, "was my continuing suspicion that 'Delay is our Most Important Product.' Not facts and understanding—just delay."

14
A Humane Solitaire

You can't play the high-stakes climate game without understanding the underlying principles. Focusing on reducing annual additions (emissions) has by now become a loser's game. But paying attention to removing CO_2 from the air will not only cancel the uncontrolled emissions but reverse overheating.

Solitaire is a great preparation for life. You lose, over and over again (in my experience, about six games in every seven). Often your access to the needed card has been closed off by a prior move—and so you learn about burning your bridges. And in many of your games, you have the slowly dawning realization that you are simply going around in a circle, making no progress. Trapped.

The earliest digital versions of solitaire were quite a shock to those accustomed to retrieving a card after laying it down on the pile. An *undo* command was quickly added.

The most recent versions of solitaire have become even more humane. They have foresight and will often tell you when you are hopelessly trapped, that there are no more moves you can make that will lead out of the maze. There are still occasions of endless loops-within-loops that the software doesn't recognize, but usually it spares you the growing despair.

Humane solitaire might be useful for providing physicians and politicians with the correct mindset. Just when they get good at the game, you take away the foresight feature. Next you take away the *undo* command. Finally you add a timer so that they lose if they merely take too long to do the right thing.

In climate science as in medicine, you become aware of irretrievable situations—say, learning that when the Amazon rain forest burns down, it won't come back for a very, very long time, quite unlike ordinary forests. Plant succession will stay stuck at grasslands, so all of that biomass will not grow back. Most of its CO_2 will remain up in the air, causing heat waves around the world. Burn locally, crash globally.

And it's bye-bye forever to perhaps half of the animal species caught up in the biggest mass extinction in the last 65 million years. Had the big drought of 1997 (or the even more serious ones in 2005, 2007, and 2010) lasted longer, we could have lost the Amazon rain forest and many of its endemic species.

We are already operating without a safety margin.

A feeling of foreboding is also increasingly common among climate scientists. While physicians are at least accustomed to patients with no moves left, the climate docs have only one patient. So when they contemplate that our profligate ways may have painted us into a corner, it is truly about the big picture, not just one person's fate.

But despair is premature. The menu of climate choices has been arbitrary pruned by the way in which the issue has been framed. When "irreversible" is used in a climate discussion, and it's not about the aforementioned ecosystem regime shifts or mass extinctions, you have to keep reminding yourself that the authors should have prefaced it with *"If we do not remove the excess CO_2 from the air,* then X is irreversible."

If you know the history of global warming science, the current framing of the climate problem was once quite logical and followed from trying to balance the budget for the physics of heat. This resulted in an intervention menu that was only about reducing emissions or reflecting more sunshine back out into space. It was only concerned with rebalancing the global mean temperature, not with drawing down the excess atmospheric CO_2 itself.

But by the turn of the century, it became clear that there is a second deadly effect of excess CO_2. In addition to the overheating, excess CO_2 acidifies the ocean surface, striking at the bottom of the food chain. So even if we stopped the rise in global mean temperature, we'd still be in big trouble.

The obvious solution to both overheating and ocean acidification is to remove the excess CO_2 from the air, stashing it into long-term storage ("carbon sequestration"). But there is very little discussion of this among the climate docs.

And in the public discussion, the great CO_2 cleanup can be confused with two other things. Once it is labeled as geoengineering (which it is), it becomes confused with one particular type of geoengineering: mimicking volcanoes by injecting sulfur in the stratosphere to reflect sunlight away from the earth. Studies now show[1] that the 1991 eruption of Mount Pinatubo in the Philippines was followed by a worldwide decrease in rainfall and river runoff, suggesting major complications might result from such attempts.

Second, drawing down atmospheric CO_2 becomes confused with scrubbing smokestack emissions to slow the growth of excess CO_2. That's not the *great* CO_2 cleanup but just another emissions reduction.

Cleaning up the excess CO_2 is analogous to what an artificial kidney does, removing the harmful molecules from the blood. What we need is the functional equivalent of the scrubbers used on submarines that remove CO_2 from the air. While plantations of scrubbers sticking up into the sky like giant fly-swatters have indeed been proposed, they would require many new zero-carbon power plants to run them. While perhaps possible, that's not quick enough.

The other way to reduce the air's excess CO_2 is to unbalance the carbon cycle, typically by preventing some of the CO_2 captured by photosynthesis from going back into the air when cells decompose. Stashing biomass where the air can't get to it is the general idea. While sealed landfills would help, it is only the ocean depths that would appear to have the capacity to house all of the new CO_2 that we have added since 1750.

The three abrupt drought steps were all surprises to the climate scientists. There was nothing in their models to predict them. Physicians cannot predict heart attacks either—but they can do a good job of preventing many of them. And what might prevent abrupt climate shifts? Getting rid of the excess CO_2 before another one happens.

In solitaire, you can always start again. It, however, is only a game.

We have three big problems—overheating, acidification, and abrupt climate shifts. It's a triple threat. Any menu of climate choices that ignores the second and third is a dangerous oversimplification. We are indeed fortunate that one set of *undo* actions—cleaning up the excess CO_2—will address all three.

15
Why Deserts Expand

Circulation changes are likely a big part of global warming's knock-on effects. The best understood is the expansion of the wet tropics and the dry subtropics over the last few decades[1]. But to understand the change in air circulation, it helps to first understand the normal "general circulation" that creates winds and waves independent of any storm system.

At the equator, the noontime sun is straight overhead. Most of the equator is over the ocean and so you'd expect the sea surface temperature to rise with global warming. And it has, since 1977. And with temperature rise, there is more evaporation, yielding higher humidity.

Warm surface air rises, creating big updrafts and thunderstorms. This air has to come back down somewhere, usually 20° to 35° north and south of the equator. During the trip the warm air cools. When cool, it is denser than the air below and so it sinks (a high-pressure zone). Air that starts out overheated travels farther before it reaches a temperature where it will sink— one reason that the tropics expand with global overheating.

The ex-tropical air comes down dry because it lost most of its water vapor on the trip up, precipitating out as rain. That's why there are usually deserts in subtropical latitudes. (The Florida peninsula escapes this fate because it has a constantly renewed source of water vapor, thanks to the warm Gulf Stream on three sides.)

In the tropics, the surface winds are usually out of the east, the so-called trade winds. When you finally get into the Temperate Zone latitudes (roughly 30° to 60° from the equator), the prevailing winds switch around to be out of the west. They carry moist ocean air over the west coast of continents.

Near the subtropical boundary—say, Mediterranean 32° latitudes—the summers are as cloud free as in the bordering deserts. It's only in the winter that storm systems coming in off the Atlantic Ocean manage to penetrate the winter-weakened high pressure systems of the Sahara and leave behind some rainfall.

This combination of winter rain and summer sun is known as a Mediterranean Climate. It is what southern California has, as well as Santiago de Chile, Perth, and Cape Town. They are all on the border of the subtropical deserts where the westerly winds begin *and* at the western edge of a continent. A rain shadow may terminate the eastward extent. Because of the mountains in Southern California, the winter rainfall may not make it as far east as Arizona. But because the Mediterranean Sea extends eastward so far, and is able to replenish the westerly's water vapor with new evaporation from the Med itself, it can produce a continent-wide Mediterranean Climate Zone.

With global overheating, big tropical updrafts may come from a
wider band of latitudes. They are not necessarily centered on the
equator—indeed, the heavy rainfall band has been shifting north
with warming[2]. And so the dry subtropics are pushed farther
away from the equator as well and that moves where the westerly
winds begin—say, from North Africa to Spain. Once its band of
winter-only rain is pushed north of the Med, there will be no
more of the en route refilling, just the rain shadow of the
Pyrenees. Southern Europe and the eastern Mediterranean
countries will be very stressed. A lot of climate refugees will be
trying to move north.

All of the places with Mediterranean climates are likely to lose
significant portions of their water supplies. Perth is building
desalination plants as quickly as it can. California is just building
more suburbs, as real-estate developers are far more influential
than climate scientists.

We don't yet know, because of insufficient records, how much
of the present expansion of the tropics has occurred gradually
and how much occurred in a stepwise manner—say, at the time of
those 1976 abrupt circulation shifts. But it is clear that any
further expansion, should it occur as suddenly as those big
drought steps in 1982 and 1997, could turn into a major
catastrophe for civilization.

16
The Worst Case Scenario

Humpty Dumpty sat on a wall,
Humpty Dumpty had a great fall.
All the King's horses,
And all the King's men
Couldn't put Humpty together again.

—traditional English nursery rhyme

It is important to analyze a worst-case scenario so that you can discover how to head it off in time—as banking and Wall Street regulators now know, having been caught in 2008 relying instead on crossed fingers.

The anthropologists show that most societies of the past have collapsed, with prolonged drought their leading cause of death[1]. So let us suppose that, sometime next year, a global-scale lurch in climate causes global-scale famine.

Actually, climate-induced famine can happen even without drought. All it took in Shakespeare's time were unseasonable summer rains that knocked down and rotted the grain crops of Europe, causing famine the following winter. When this kept happening year after year, scapegoats were sought and witch-burning became very popular in Switzerland and Germany. This was promoted both by climate change and the need of leaders to be seen "doing something about the problem." The deadly fad swept westward as far as Massachusetts before fading a century later.

While bad droughts happen all the time without a collapse of civilization, note that we're now talking about a global climate shift—like 1997 but bigger—and not the usual regional drought where you might still import food from, or take refuge in, a neighboring country. Most countries would get into trouble at about the same time, overwhelming aid organizations. Now it's your neighbor's kids who look emaciated and are going door to door, begging for food.

Urban food riots would follow. Police and fire departments would be overwhelmed. People would flee the cities to escape the disorder and seek food.

It's not merely that you can't go home again. Should you become separated from family and friends in the crowd, you would find yourself alone in a mob of hungry strangers. Climate refugees suffer war, famine, pestilence, and genocide—even today.

But in an event so widespread, this death spiral would draw in most people in most places. It would be especially bad in countries like the United States where only one percent of the people live close to the food supply. (Even in a farm state such as Iowa, only four percent live on farms.) The rest of us reside at the end of a long, and easily diverted, just-in-time supply line. The bigger the urban concentration, the harder it would collapse.

The human population could crash, taking most of civilization with it—almost everything that we and our predecessors have worked so hard to achieve.

And in case you don't know what a 90 percent population crash looks like, let me describe the one for birds on Pacific islands during the 1982 El Niño when ocean productivity collapsed from the surface overheating (plankton prefer cooler water). First, the adults couldn't find enough food to feed the hungry mouths in the nest. Nestlings were abandoned because, as the parents ranged more widely in search of food, a day came when they couldn't even find enough food to power their own return trip to the nest. Then 90 percent of the adults died as the famine persisted.

The famine has persisted for decades because the sea surface temperatures have remained elevated, hitting at the bottom of the food chain. Visit Easter Island today and the first thing you notice is that the water is clear and lifeless. The few fishing boats that are left are now specializing in deep-water fish such as tuna. There are a few sea birds left but that's because some mountain lakes serve as rest stops for long over-ocean migrations.

Humans are smarter than birds but something similar is likely to happen if a sudden climate shift ruins fishing and agricultural productivity for long enough that cities collapse. Whatever you might think about the Earth already having too many humans to support, remember the dynamics of a population crash. Survivors would cluster into groups sharing terrible memories, hating all of the neighboring groups for good reasons, constantly obsessed with revenge or being on the receiving end of revenge.

That is considerably worse than Hobbes' state of nature where life is "solitary, poor, nasty, brutish, and short."

Do you really think that civilized values will still function, given such a state of affairs? Ethical behavior? Empathy and giving? Protection from predators? Tolerance and civility? A safety net for the unfortunate? Conservation? Government respectful of the people? If climate stability goes, nearly all of the other values could go too. All within a decade or two.

Climate trumps all. But none of this is inevitable—just increasingly probable if we do not undertake a crash program (as in *The Great CO2 Cleanup*) for removing the excess CO2 from the air.

Acknowledgements

I am grateful to James J. Anderson, David Archer, John Edwards, Steve Emerson, Richard Gammon, Katherine Graubard, Charles Laird, Edward Miles, James Murray, Gary Odell, Gordon Orians, Julian Sachs, Eric Steig, Alan Trimble, Arthur Whiteley, and Dennis Willows for scientific discussions. For improving the readability of the manuscript, I am particularly grateful to Larry S. Anderson and Peter Rockas.

Chapter Notes

Chapter 1   **An Inventory of Trouble**

2   Richard B. Alley, et al (2002) Abrupt Climate Change: Inevitable Surprises. U.S. National Research Council.

Peter U. Clark, et al (2008) Abrupt Climate Change. A report by the U.S. Climate Change Science Program and the Subcommittee on Global Change Research. U.S. Geological Survey, Reston, VA, 459 pp.

3   See Figure 2.

4   Dai A, Trenberth KE, Qian T (2004) A global data set of Palmer Drought Severity Index for 1870–2002: Relationship with soil moisture and effects of surface warming. J Hydrometeorology 5:1117-1130. www.cgd.ucar.edu/cas/adai/papers/Dai_pdsi_paper.pdf with a 2006 update at www.tiimes.ucar.edu/highlights/fy06/images/global_land_dry_conditions.jpg.

5   Marengo J, et al (2008) The drought of Amazonia in 2005. J Climate 21:495–516. DOI:10.1175/2007JCLI1600.1

Phillips OL, et al (2009) Drought sensitivity of the Amazon rainforest. Science 323:1344–1347. DOI: 10.1126/science.1164033

Santilli M, Moutinho P, Schwartzman S, Nepstad D, Curran L, Nobre C (2005) Tropical deforestation and the Kyoto protocol. Climatic Change 71:267–276.

6   Simon L. Lewis, Paulo M. Brando, Oliver L. Phillips, Geertje M. F. van der
    Heijden, and Daniel Nepstad (2011) The 2010 Amazon Drought. *Science*
    331:554. DOI:10.1126/science.1200807

    Xu, L., A. Samanta, M. H. Costa, S. Ganguly, R. R. Nemani, and R. B. Myneni
    (2011), Widespread decline in greenness of Amazonian vegetation due to the
    2010 drought, *Geophys. Res. Lett.*, 38, L07402,
    DOI:10.1029/2011GL046824.

7   Schlosser P, Bönisch G, Rhein M, Bayer R (1991) Reduction of deepwater
    formation in the Greenland Sea during the 1980s: Evidence from tracer data.
    Science 251:1054–1056.
    www.sciencemag.org/cgi/reprint/251/4997/1054.pdf

8   Rhines PB (2006) Sub-Arctic oceans and global climate. *Weather* 61:109-
    118. DOI:10.1256/wea.223.05

    Våge K, et al (2009) Surprising return of deep convection to the subpolar
    North Atlantic Ocean in winter 2007–2008. *Nature Geoscience* 2:67–72.
    DOI:10.1038/ngeo382.

9   Joshi M, Hawkins E, Sutton E, Lowe J, Frame D (2011) Projections of
    when temperature change will exceed 2°C above pre-industrial levels.
    Nature Climate Change 1:407-412. doi:10.1038/nclimate1261

Chapter 2   *Discovering Global Fever*

1   Frank Capra (1958) The unchained goddess. Video at
    www.youtube.com/watch?v=m-AXBbuDxRY.

2   Most of this history can be found in Spencer R. Weart (2003) *The Discovery
    of Global Warming*. Harvard University Press. Updated version at
    www.aip.org/history/climate.

3   Caldeira K, Wickett ME (2003) Anthropogenic carbon and ocean. *Nature*
    425:365. DOI:10.1038/425365a.

4   Stefan Rahmstorf, et al. (2007) Recent climate observations compared to
    projections. *Science* 316:709. DOI:10.1126/science.1136843.

5   I owe much of my appreciation of risk to my father, Fred H. Calvin (1909-
    1979), who was a senior insurance executive in charge of pricing premiums;
    as we drove around town, he frequently pointed out risky situations and told
    a story of what happened to someone in a similar circumstance.

    A good history is Peter L. Bernstein (1996) *Against the Gods: The*

Remarkable Story of Risk. Wiley.

Chapter 3   *The Climate Docs*

1   Christakis NA, Lamont EB (2000) Extent and determinants of error in doctors' prognoses in terminally ill patients: prospective cohort study. *BMJ* 19:469–473.

2   Calvin WH (2012) *The Great CO2 Cleanup: Backing Out of the Danger Zone.* Amazon.

Chapter 4   *How Much Time Do We Have Left?*

1   *See* Figure 2C.

2   Miller AJ, Cayan DR, Barnett TP, Oberhuber JM (1994) The 1976-77 climate shift of the Pacific Ocean. *Oceanography* 7: 21–26. meteora.ucsd.edu/~miller/papers/shift.html

3   It is well established that, since the late 1970s, there has been a poleward shift of the Sahara and other Hadley Cell deserts and of the eddy-driven jet streams and their storm tracks. Almost all of the global climate models predict that increasing greenhouse gas concentrations will cause the trend to continue throughout the 21st century. See the 2007 IPCC report and Kidston, J., and E. P. Gerber (2010) Intermodel variability of the poleward shift of the austral jet stream in the CMIP3 integrations linked to biases in 20th century climatology, *Geophysical Research Letters,* 37, L09708, doi:10.1029/2010GL042873.

Chapter 5   *Underestimating Climate*

4   Wolter K, Timlin MS (1998) Measuring the strength of ENSO events: How does 1997/98 rank? *Weather* 53:315-323.

4   Thompson DWJ, Kennedy JJ, Wallace JM, Jones PD (2008) A large discontinuity in the mid-twentieth century in observed global-mean surface temperature. *Nature* 453:646-649, DOI:10.1038/nature06982.

5   Dai A, Trenberth KE, Qian T (2004) A global data set of Palmer Drought Severity Index for 1870–2002: Relationship with soil moisture and effects of surface warming. *J Hydrometeorology* 5:1117-1130. www.cgd.ucar.edu/cas/adai/papers/Dai_pdsi_paper.pdf with a 2006

update at
www.tiimes.ucar.edu/highlights/fy06/images/global_land_dry_condi
tions.jpg.

[6]   Miller AJ, Cayan DR, Barnett TP, Oberhuber JM (1994) The 1976-77 climate
shift of the Pacific Ocean. *Oceanography* 7: 21–26.
meteora.ucsd.edu/~miller/papers/shift.html

[1]   I spent the first third of my career studying nonlinear systems from the
biophysical side of neurobiology and have long remarked on how similar the
abrupt climate shifts of the last ice age are in appearance to the heart cell's
three-phase action potential (sudden depolarization, gradual repolarization,
then fast repolarization). The three-phase Dansgaard-Oeschger events
(sudden rewarming, gradual cooling, then abrupt cooling) from the last ice
age that Ganopolski and Rahmstorf analyze serve to illustrate how similar
the two nonlinear oscillators may be in their state transitions.

Andrey Ganopolski, Stefan Rahmstorf (2002) Abrupt glacial climate changes
due to stochastic resonance. *Physical Review Letters*
doi:10.1103/PhysRevLett.88.038501.

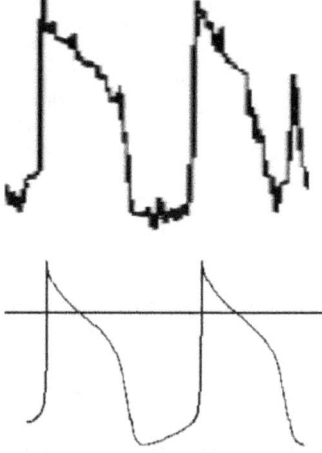

Top: Dansgaard-Oeschger events #20 and #19 between 80,000 and 70,000
years ago, magnified from Figure 3.
Bottom: Two cardiac action potentials from a guinea pig ventricle cell (two
seconds total).

2   Joe Romm (2008) at climateprogress.org/2008/09/30/why-scientists-arent-more-persuasive-part-1/

3   Mark Bowen (2005) *Thin Ice*. Henry Holt and Co.

Chapter 6   *Speaking Too Softly*

4   Paul Krugman (2011) *http://nyti.ms/f4DCcp*

1   Feinberg M, Willer R (2011) Apocalypse Soon? Dire Messages Reduce Belief in Global Warming by Contradicting Just-World Beliefs. *Psychological Science* 22: 34-38, doi:10.1177/0956797610391911.

    Markowitz EM, Shariff AF (2012) Climate change and moral judgment. *Nature Climate Change* 2:243-247. DOI 10.1038/nclimate1378

2   Kevin Schaefer, Tingjun Zhang, Lori Bruhwiler, Andrew P. Barrett (2011) Amount and timing of permafrost carbon release in response to climate warming. *Tellus*, doi:10.1111/j.1600-0889.2011.00527.x

3   Christakis NA, Lamont EB (2000) Extent and determinants of error in doctors' prognoses in terminally ill patients: prospective cohort study. *BMJ* 19:469–473.

4   *Warning* of an eclipse of the sun now involves wonderfully precise times and locations. But back before Isaac Newton learned how to calculate the trajectories, it was possible to issue a warning long before the bright sun became dim enough to spot the crescent shape of the eclipse in progress. All it took was a multifaceted jewel, held near a window, reflecting little images of the crescent sun on nearby walls (the pinhole camera principle). Outdoors, one holds a leaf with a small hole in it so that it casts a shadow on one's chest. One looks at the little bright spot within the leaf's shadow and sees if it has become a crescent. Lacking a holy leaf, you can cross your fingers to produce a small opening.

    And one could probabilisticly *predict* the night of a lunar eclipse with no technology at all. About two-thirds of all lunar eclipses occur on either the 6th or 12th full moon following an observed eclipse. To become known as someone with a direct line to whomever runs the heavens, just keep a count and announce your prediction weeks ahead of time. You can even profit from frequently being wrong: just tell everyone to pray to stop the eclipse. Often this will seem to work. And on the occasions when only a partial eclipse occurs, they might believe that their prayers or ceremonies prevented the dreaded full eclipse. See William H. Calvin (1991) *How the Shaman Stole the Moon*. Bantam.

5   www.nytimes.com/2011/03/17/world/asia/17nuclear.html

Chapter 7   *Low-Ball Estimates*

1   William H. Calvin (1986) *The River that Flows Uphill.* Macmillian. Revised edition (2010).

2   *See* Figure 3 and Richard Alley (2000) *The Two-Mile Time Machine,* Princeton University Press.

3   I discuss the climate chattering's implications for human evolution in <u>A Brain for All Seasons</u> (2002) and <u>A Brief History of the Mind</u> (2004).

Chapter 8   *Raising an Uncertain Alarm*

1   Lisa Sanders (2009) *Every Patient Tells a Story: Medical Mysteries and the Art of Diagnosis.* Random House. "In medicine, uncertainty is the water we swim in. The chance of being wrong is overwhelming when dealing with something more complicated than a sore throat."

Chapter 9   Core Values and Climate Roulette

Chapter 10   *Climate Surprises Since 1976*

1   Miller AJ, Cayan DR, Barnett TP, Oberhuber JM (1994) The 1976-77 climate shift of the Pacific Ocean. *Oceanography* 7: 21–26. *meteora.ucsd.edu/~miller/papers/shift.html*

2   Jet stream shifts, *see* the 2007 IPCC report and Kidston, J., and E. P. Gerber (2010) Intermodel variability of the poleward shift of the austral jet stream in the CMIP3 integrations linked to biases in 20th century climatology, *Geophys. Res. Lett.,* 37, L09708, DOI:<u>10.1029/2010GL042873</u>.

3   *See* Figure 2B.

4   *See* Figure 4.

5   *See* Figure 2A.

6   *See* Figure 2C.

7   Robine J-M et al. (2008). Death toll exceeded 70,000 in Europe during the summer of 2003. <u>Comptes Rendus Biologies,</u> 331(2):171–8.

Bettina Menne, Franziska Matthies, eds. (2009) Improving public health responses to extreme weather/heat-waves –<u>EuroHEAT</u>. World Health

Organization.

[8] You are already familiar with two changes of state—when ice thaws to a liquid, which with further heating can evaporate to become a vapor. But a steplike change of state need not show up in climate data as a step.
Those who know some calculus might recall that the step is the time integral of the pulse; integrate the step and you get a ramp—and conversely that the time derivative of the ramp is a step, that of the step is a pulse. What is observable as climate may also be the derivative or integral of an underlying steplike change of state.

Chapter 11   *Figuring the Odds*

[1] Cunningham SA, Marsh R (2010) Observing and modeling changes in the Atlantic MOC. *WIREs Clim Change* 1:180–191. DOI: 10.1002/wcc.22

[2] Schlosser P, Bönisch G, Rhein M, Bayer R (1991) Reduction of deepwater formation in the Greenland Sea during the 1980s: Evidence from tracer data. *Science* 251:1054–1056.
www.sciencemag.org/cgi/reprint/251/4997/1054.pdf

[3] Rhines PB (2006) Sub-Arctic oceans and global climate. *Weather* 61:109-118. DOI: 10.1256/wea.223.05

[4] Våge K, et al (2009) Surprising return of deep convection to the subpolar North Atlantic Ocean in winter 2007–2008. *Nature Geoscience* 2:67–72. DOI:10.1038/ngeo382.

Chapter 12   *Is "Stabilizing" False Advertising?*

[1] But 560 ppm is quite arbitrary; it's just that 19th-century scientists liked to talk of doubling time as a stand-in for rate.

Chapter 13   The Education of a Climate Consultant

Chapter 14   *A Humane Solitaire*

[1] Naomi Oreskes, Erik Conway (2010) *Merchants of Doubt: How a Handful of Scientists Obscured the Truth on Issues from Tobacco Smoke to Global Warming.* Bloomsbury Press.

Eric Pooley (2010) *The Climate War: True Believers, Power Brokers, and the Fight to Save the Earth.* Hyperon.

[2] James Powell (2011) *The Inquisition of Climate Science.* Columbia

University Press.

[1]   K. E. Trenberth, Aiguo Dai (2007), Effects of Mount Pinatubo volcanic eruption on the hydrological cycle as an analog of geoengineering, *Geophys. Res. Lett.*, 34, L15702, DOI:10.1029/2007GL030524.

Chapter 15   *Why Deserts Expand*

[1]   Seidel DJ, Fu Q, Randel WJ, Reichler TJ (2008) Widening of the tropical belt in a changing climate. *Nature Geoscience* 1:21–24.

[2]   Julian P. Sachs, Conor L. Myhrvold (2011) A shifting band of rain. *Scientfic American,* March:60-65.

Chapter 16   *The Worst Case Scenario*

[1]   Diamond J. (2003) *Collapse: How Societies Choose to Succeed or Fail.* New York: Viking.